WHAT
IN
THE
ACTUAL
FUCK

By Rachel Gitlevich

For my Grandma, Yulia —
Thank you for being like a second mom to me. For all our spelling bees during car rides, for cheering me on in every dream I pursued, from college to business, and beyond. You've always been my angel, first by my side and now from above. I carry your love with me, always.

There is a voice beneath the noise,
a knowing beneath the pain.
You are not lost.
Even when the world taught you to forget,
your soul remembers the way home.

—Rachel Gitlevitch

TABLE OF CONTENTS

CHAPTER ONE 13

CHAPTER TWO 24

CHAPTER THREE..34

CHAPTER FOUR 44

CHAPTER FIVE...53

CHAPTER SIX 64

CHAPTER SEVEN 71

CHAPTER EIGHT 82

CHAPTER NINE...90

CHAPTER TEN...97

CHAPTER ELEVEN..103

EPILOGUE.. 110

ACKNOWLEDGMENTS..112

RESOURCES 114

ADDITIONAL RESOURCES 119

INTRODUCTION

TODAY, AS I WRITE THIS, I can see what a gift it is to have been granted the opportunity to incarnate on earth. It's been quite a journey to arrive at that point of view, and some days, I'll admit, I still struggle to see it that way. I imagine that at times you, like me, question your purpose, your potential, or what you've been placed here to do. You might look at some people and think, *"Wow, they really have their shit together."* But let's be real, none of us really do. We're all just figuring it out along the way.

I'm writing this book for me and for you. I'm writing it to shine a light on how, despite the chaotic mess that life often throws our way, there's an undeniable beauty woven through it all.

We all share an inescapable relationship with life. Some of us hate it, some of us love it, and many of us maintain a love-hate relationship with life. Regardless of how we feel, life is the common thread that binds us all. As much as we try, at times, to keep a stronghold grip on life to influence outcomes, we simply have little control over the twists and turns of our existence. Our best attempts at outsmarting the unpredictability, thinking we can somehow bend it to our will are generally futile. Yet, as Danna Faulds puts it: "There is no controlling life. Allow, and grace will carry you to higher ground."

For a long time, the concept of allowance was elusive to me, and I struggled to accept that life simply is. There are no inherently good or bad experiences; there are only experiences. It's up to us to choose how we relate to them. We don't judge the ocean for having a current. We might try to fight the waves, but the easiest way to swim is to stop resisting and instead flow with the tide.

In the chapters that follow, I'll delve into why I've chosen to embrace life, no matter the outcomes. Rather than offering you a perfectly polished narrative, though, I'm going to present more of a raw testament to resilience, allowance, and the feeling of home that we can find within.

When you think of home, what comes up for you? Do you think of it as a place of comfort, where the walls have witnessed your laughter and tears? Or does the idea of home carry a weight, a space you've wanted to escape, where the air feels too heavy to breathe? In the past, have you truly felt safe at home, or has that feeling of safety been elusive for you?

Wherever you are on your path, I'm sharing my story so you know you're not alone. By turning these pages, we're beginning a journey toward something deeper, a feeling of safety that comes from within. We'll explore what it means to feel at home, not through walls or addresses, but in the bodies and lives we already carry.

If you're reading this, it means you've been granted a meat suit, or as some might call it, a body. It's ours to inhabit, to understand, and to embrace. To experience the full spectrum of emotions. To cry, to laugh, and to do our best job, not to judge ourselves. The road isn't always easy, and as you'll read in the coming pages, some days my body has felt like the last place I wanted to be. But my hope is that, by the end of this journey, I can share a map of sorts, that will help with finding a way to welcome ourselves back home.

Your identity does not reside in your trauma or your wounds. These are chapters in your story, not the title of your book. They are experiences you've had, not definitions of who you are. While they may have shaped you, they do not have the power to own you, unless you let them. You are so much more than the pain you've carried or the scars you bear.

However, it is your responsibility to heal, and that doesn't involve erasing the past but rather, reclaiming your power from it. It's about tending to your wounds with compassion and courage, acknowledging their existence without allowing them to dictate your future. No one else can take this journey for you. The road to healing can feel lonely. The good news is, you do not have to walk it alone.

By taking responsibility for your healing, you step into the wholeness of your being, choosing growth over stagnation. It's not an easy path, it rarely is, but it's a worthwhile one. In healing, you discover that your identity is not the pain you've felt, but the person you become as you rise from the ashes—

"When we dig in the ashes, we find one ember, and very gently we fan that ember, blow on it, it gets brighter, and from that ember we rebuild the fire. The only thing that's important is that ember."
—*Ram Dass*

I wrestled with getting started writing this book. I imagined I would wake up one night, magically inspired, and write it all in a single, fluid sweep under the shining light of a full moon. Maybe I was afraid of fully confronting my story, or perhaps I feared the emotional upheaval it might stir. But here I am, discovering unexpected solace in the act of writing.

If you're sitting on the idea of your own story, waiting for the perfect moment or for life to slow down, I want you to keep in mind that life doesn't have a pause or rewind button. If you have an idea, even a tiny spark, I encourage you to make time to write. Your voice matters. Your story matters.

I never thought of myself as a writer. Yet, here I am, having found my way through the maze of self-doubt and fear. To reach this point, I had to deeply connect with my reasons for writing. I had to understand that sharing my story could, in itself, be a powerful way to process all I have been through. I hope that it will resonate with you on some level as well, and that you will feel inspired to confront your own life experiences and perhaps find gratitude where you may not have felt it before.

Am I asking you to find gratitude for all the challenges life throws your way? Absolutely not, because let's face it, life can be incredibly intense or unhinged sometimes. However, even when life feels like a relentless pile of... chaos, it's also an opportunity to learn, grow, and discover the beauty. Because when we take a moment to look and become present, we can find clarity. Whatever storm you may be weathering, keep in mind, it will not last forever. There is a light after every storm, and it's our job to return to the light over and over and over again. To find our way home.

1

∞

I'D JUST OPENED MY LAPTOP and was about to jump on a coaching call when my phone lit up with an incoming call from Dr. Patterson's office. We had been playing phone tag for days, with each missed call adding a layer of anxiety. Her first call had come in after hours, and though I'd immediately returned her call, I reached the office without getting any answers. I reassured myself that a missed call from my doctor couldn't be anything too alarming, right? After all, I was 27 and invincible, or so I believed. Life was meant to be lived in the moment, to be spent dancing with friends and chasing dreams.

For years, that heart-shaped mole on my shoulder had been a minor footnote in my health history. My mom had urged me to get it checked out, convinced it had started to look suspicious.

In 2016, a dermatologist took a quick look and told me it was fine, that it was something to keep an eye on but not to worry about. To me, that meant it was nothing to worry about. Moles didn't grow overnight; they took time to change, and my last checkup had confirmed everything was normal.

So, when I saw the 10-digit number flash across my screen, I answered with a squeaky, nervous hello.

"Hi, Rachel—it's Dr. Patterson. How are you?"

"I'm doing all right, how are you?"

"I'm all right. So, we received your pathology results..." Her calm tone of voice seemed almost surreal as she delivered the devastating news. "It's melanoma."

Melanoma?

The word hit my ears like a heavy, foreign language. I scrambled to type it into Google, the search results instantly flooding my screen with horrifying images and confusing medical jargon that was far beyond my grasp. My throat went dry, and my mind spun as I tried to grasp the gravity of what I'd heard.

"I'm sorry, what?" I managed to croak, in a voice that was rough and barely coherent.

"Rachel—it's skin cancer."

Dr. Patterson began outlining my options, next steps, specialists, and potential treatments. But her words ran together, blurring into a distant echo. With shaking hands, I scribbled notes on a sticky pad, a messy, illegible scrawl. It felt like a cruel trick, a foreign script, all pointing to a harsh reality I desperately wanted to refuse. In part of my mind, I found myself critiquing my own reaction. Shouldn't I be crying, praying, or reaching for solace in some form of divine intervention? My body had other ideas, though, and there were no dramatic tears, no spiritual epiphany.

Instead, when I finished the call, I could do little more than stare into space and grapple with my new reality. It felt like a mistake; maybe my pathology results had been accidentally swapped with someone else's. There was no cinematic moment of grief shared with a best friend, no comforting embrace from a family member, and no partner reassuring me that I'd be okay.

The reality of my diagnosis was starkly devoid of romanticism. I sat alone, in shock, trying to swallow the fact that my life had just changed irrevocably. I couldn't cry. I felt utterly paralyzed.

After I moved through the initial days of processing, I found myself seized by a determination to take action. My emotional fog persisted, though, and I leaned on my closest friends for support. I quickly scheduled several consultations and was thankful to have my best friend Eliza accompany me to my first specialist appointment with Dr. Pae, who would eventually perform the surgery to remove my melanoma. The consultation visit went by in a blur; I felt barely there, the doctor's remark that I should prepare for a scar resembling a 'shark bite' landing in the most surreal way.

Looking back at how my cancer journey began unfolding, I see it as a testament to the power of choice and resilience. In every decision I made, and every step I took, I was driven by an inner strength I had little idea I even possessed. That strength is what got me through the years to come; my journey of becoming would test me in ways I had never anticipated.

In the time leading up to that first surgery, I spent my days pretty much just going through the motions. Nighttime was when anxiety would creep in to keep me company. My mind pulsed with the push and pull of uncertainty, and my desire to avoid what was coming, this internal battle with the urge to just get it over with.

When the day arrived and I traveled with my mom along quiet, early morning streets to the hospital, I noticed that I did not feel afraid. Rather than fear, my mind dwelled on the question of what I "should" be thinking and feeling in this very serious situation. I was about to be put under and cut open, shouldn't I feel more afraid? Why did this feel so surreal? I was struck by the contrast between the gravity of what was unfolding for me versus the normalcy of what was a routine day for the hospital staff. I conversed with nurses and nodded "no" when the anesthesiologist asked if I had any questions. I couldn't think of anything to ask. All my mind could conjure was a thought that I kept to myself: "My life is literally in your hands."

I was wheeled into the operating room and the buzz of pre-surgery soon enveloped me, murmured medical jargon, the rhythmic beeping of monitors, and the chill of a sterile environment. The nurses and technicians moved with practiced efficiency, initiating my IV and posing a rapid-fire sequence of questions about my medical history and any allergies to anesthesia. With each question, I felt pulled further into a world I wanted desperately to steer clear of. The anesthesiologist entered, and with him a calm presence. Before I knew it, he had me counting down from five, as though summoning the last vestiges of consciousness before surrendering to the veil of anesthesia.

Then, in what seemed like an instant, I was waking up in the recovery room, again listening to the gentle hum of medical equipment. My upper back felt sore, a dull ache reminding me of the operation, though it was more of a distant awareness. The pain was dulled by what anesthesia still lingered in my system. The recovery room was a blur of soft voices and the occasional clink of a medical instrument, but as much as I wanted to lie back and rest, a pressing issue soon made itself known: an overwhelming urge to pee.

I gathered the courage to tell a nurse, who had just asked, "Water or juice?" that I needed to pee. She gently informed me that standing or walking was not yet an option and offered a bedpan as an alternative. Hesitant, but in desperate need of relief, I consented, and she carefully placed a bedpan beneath me. I began to relieve myself and felt an uncomfortable splash against my butt. My face flushed and my heart began to race with the sudden worry that the bedpan might overflow. The thought of a shameful, uncontainable mess in the recovery room made me nervous.

I tried calling for help, but my voice was weak as I repeated, "Hello? Helloo? Help?" The seconds stretched into what felt like an eternity before the nurse finally reappeared, holding her calm demeanor intact as she asked if I was finished. Embarrassed but relieved, I assured her that I was done. It was nothing but a minor crisis, one managed with professional grace, but it left me feeling exhausted and vulnerable, on top of the disorientation of recovery. This was little more than a first hint of the powerlessness I would soon come to experience with an unwelcome level of frequency.

The healing process, I would learn, was far from smooth. My back began to rebel against the dissolvable stitches. They seemed to have no intention of disappearing as promised. Despite my skin's earnest attempts to heal over, the stitches continued to stubbornly poke through its surface. Every time I felt a twinge of discomfort at the site of my incision, every time I maneuvered to look at my back in the mirror, I felt like my body was shouting, "*Absolutely not,*" pushing away the promise of recovery and complicating the process with a layer of discomfort and frustration.

It appeared my body was resisting the healing process, and the sight of those stubborn stitches protruding from my skin soon became a symbol of the slow and often unpredictable nature of recovery. It was a painful lesson, one that taught me healing is rarely straightforward. Patience would need to be my constant companion as I navigated through days of uneven progress and unexpected setbacks.

When my pathology results came in, they delivered news that felt like everything we wanted to hear: "The wide area excision and sentinel node biopsy had yielded clean margins." I was euphoric, my cancer was out, and I was, in that moment, "cured!" It felt like the universe had handed me a golden ticket, a VIP pass to a world where cancer was nothing more than a distant memory. I would soon face the sobering realization that my tangle with cancer was far from over.

In the months following my surgery, I found myself coping with a new reality, one that included constant fear and uncertainty. Everything felt different. On one hand, I had simply gone through a fairly routine surgery, but on the other, I had just come face to face with my mortality. While I had gotten the "all clear," there were no guarantees. It was no more than a temporary reprieve, really, because it could come back at any time. It felt strange that the world carried on as usual, while I was still dealing with something so intense, both physically and emotionally. I've read that 1 in 3 people will face some kind of cancer in their lives, meaning most people will face something similar to my experience, or will have supported someone who has, and yet, no one seemed to be talking about it. Everything seemed like it was business as usual, and that was hard to wrap my head around.

I found myself slipping into unhealthy coping mechanisms. I had trusted my own body for over two decades, and I found myself questioning how cancer had come onto the scene. Had I betrayed my body in some way, or had it betrayed me? I blamed myself and my own choices more than my body, and I began to feel like an unwelcome guest in my own body. What better way to deal with that than to try and escape it? I drank more and partied harder as I tried to drown out the dark reality of my health condition.

That same summer, I stumbled into a new relationship. One that went from zero to one hundred real quick. It was like a summer romance on steroids, intense, over-the-top, and filled with empty promises. Within weeks of meeting this man, he declared, "I want to marry you and for you to have my babies." If I hadn't been so deeply infatuated and high on the attention, I would have seen his grand gestures as the red flags they were. He seemed to be operating straight from a playbook on love-bombing. He called me "the one," suggested we move in together after a month, and regularly sent me lavish flower bouquets. Despite hardly knowing him, his declarations of undying love made me feel wanted and chosen. At the time, I thought that gave me a feeling of safety. I mean, he had never given me a reason not to trust him.

In the midst of this relationship, I attended the Lewis Howes' Summit of Greatness, a self-help conference that marked an inner turning point. Surrounded by inspiring individuals, I began to tap into my inner strength in a way I hadn't done in a long time. In the stories of growth and personal triumph I heard that weekend, I absorbed important messages about the profound power of choice and the importance of staying true to myself. I reflected on my drinking and realized I was walking a slippery slope. My dad was an alcoholic, and I knew that if I continued with this behavior, I might not be able to find my way back. I made a conscious choice to give up drinking.

That choice didn't sit all that well with my over-the-top boyfriend, however. Although he said he supported my decision to stop drinking, his actions didn't play out that way. When I refused his offer of a glass of wine one night, he whined, *"Where's fun Rachel?"* And so, as quickly as our relationship had started, it began to unravel just as fast. After a two-month rollercoaster ride of emotions, he ended things. Delivering the crushing news not in the comfort of a cozy café with a quiet conversation, but rather in the park, in the pouring rain, on a bleacher bench.

After he left, I sat, drenched to the bone, with my hoodie plastered to my head, and tried to process the abrupt end to our whirlwind romance. I couldn't help but think, *"What in the actual fuck?"* This wasn't the rosy romantic comedy I'd been looking for. Instead, I felt as though I'd just experienced the climactic scene of a tragic opera. The rain hit my face, mixing with my tears, and I faced the harsh truth: this wasn't the love story I had desperately hoped it to be. It seemed I'd been "unlucky" in love for as long as I could remember.

In a way, my first love kind of broke me. I had been just 21 and he was 10 years older. When we first met in a neighborhood bar, he'd been dating someone else, but I had such a crush on him that we stayed in touch while I spent six months in Australia. We sent postcards and letters to each other, and a couple of months into my study abroad program, he wrote that things with the person he'd been seeing didn't work out. On my way home, I made a pitstop in Thailand to reunite with my best friend, where we spent 36 hours together. In that moment, I realized how homesick I was. So, instead of staying an additional week exploring Thailand, I rerouted my flight to come home a week early. It's funny how the timing of the universe works. Had I not cut my trip short, or made a different choice, every little synchronistic moment that followed would have created a different outcome. Who knows if I would have ended up dating my first love.

Upon my arrival home, I was greeted with hugs by my two roommates, and craving some Chicago-style deep dish, we made our way downtown to Giordano's. After our meal, we boarded the subway, or "el," and that's when I saw him. There he was, casually dressed in a black hoodie, in the exact train car we were stepping into, the man I'd had a crush on all summer. I hopped into his lap, and it wasn't long before we began seeing each other.

In hindsight, I can see our relationship was punctuated by gaslighting, but at the time I was too wrapped up in the intensity of our physical connection to see it clearly. I never judged him, and he took that being in allowance of him for granted. One night when I wasn't feeling well, I asked him to drop by for snuggles and soup, but he made excuses, saying things like "he couldn't afford to get sick." He handed me chicken soup at my doorway, like he was afraid to come any closer, as if I were poisonous. Somehow, that almost made me feel worse. The next day, I stayed home from work, still feeling the sting of our argument. I started wondering if maybe I had been unreasonable, if I had asked for too much. I wished he had stayed. I wished things had gone differently.

He called me the next day and told me that after he left my place, he went to the bar. That news dropped a pit in my stomach. It felt like he had chosen the bar over me, and it wasn't the first time. Still, I somehow took it as if it were my fault. He called twice while he was at work to check in, and part of me held onto that as a sign he cared. I decided to leave a pie in his kitchen for him to find after work. It was Pi Day, after all. Even though I was hurting, I wanted to show him that I was still choosing him.

As I approached his apartment door, I noticed the lights were on, which seemed strange. When I unlocked the door and stepped inside, I heard a woman's voice. I immediately ran out and called his phone. When he picked up, he sounded a little frazzled.

"Hi, what's up?"

"Um, hi babe, are you home?"

"No, I'm at work, why?"

"I felt bad about our fight last night, felt like I was the one that caused you to go to the bar, so I wanted to leave you a sweet dessert for you to come home to," I replied, "but then I noticed the lights were on and I heard a female voice. Did you leave the TV on or something?"

"Um, yeah I left the TV on. That's so sweet of you to bring me dessert. I can just swing by your place on my way home to grab it," he said.

"Why would you swing by when I'm right here? I can just leave it for you," I answered. "So, you're at work?" I asked again.

"Yes," he replied, and I hung up the phone and waltzed back into his place.

I made my way down the few steps into his apartment where I was greeted by what I'll generously call his "side piece," who approached with a deer-in-headlights expression, hands raised as though I was about to pounce. I assured her, "I promise I'm not here to hurt you. I would just like some answers." She continued keeping her distance as I approached, and we began to chitchat. Finally, I asked the unavoidable question, "When the two of you were together in California, did you sleep together?" Her reply, "Do you want him to tell you or me?" was all the confirmation I needed; I left the pie on his kitchen counter and slammed the door on my way out.

He had mentioned a few months prior that he'd be traveling to a work conference in California with a co-worker we'll call Marnie. He assured me they'd be in different hotel rooms, and that she had a boyfriend, so I had nothing to worry about. When I found her inside his apartment that day, my intuitive feeling was confirmed. He'd been lying all along. That knowledge was everything I needed to break up with him, but still, it was tough. He was like my Kryptonite. I knew he wasn't good for me, but it was hard to let go of feeling loved, not to mention the headiness of our physical intimacy, and my hope for a potential future together. For years he tried to get me back, and while I resisted, I struggled to trust anyone after that.

From there, I started dating guys who today I would recognize as "emotionally unavailable." Though I can see now that I was the common denominator in that pattern, I couldn't see it then. I had difficulty opening my heart, and then when I did and it didn't work out, I would tell myself, *"I told you so."* I started dating a wealthy young man from Luxembourg who I'd met at a Moby concert years earlier. Over the course of two years, he would stay with me for several weeks at a time, and then I would travel to Europe to visit him. Our relationship had a magical, fairy tale-like air. I met his family at their summer home in the

South of France, and the two of us explored the area's beaches and coastal villages together.

When he moved to Chicago to enroll in a graduate studies program, though, I began to notice how his wealthy upbringing had turned him into someone who needed a ton of help with figuring out life. On top of being his girlfriend, it seemed he wanted me to be a parent, guide, therapist, and coach, and I couldn't possibly fulfill all those roles. Things unraveled within the space of the next few months, and I found myself alone once again.

When my love-bomber left me sitting on that bench in the rain, lamenting the end of another failed attempt at romance, I knew I had to stop trying to escape the realities of my life by losing myself in love. I knew I no longer wanted to distract myself with alcohol, and now I was able to see that losing myself in the distraction of a head-over-heels relationship was no different. Absent that distraction, I was forced to once again confront the uncertain realities around my health. This time, however, I did not try to escape the dark thoughts. The things I had learned about inner strength and resilience sat at the forefront of my mind, and I found comfort thinking about the power of allowance. As much as the sting of rejection hurt, I knew it was discomfort that would force me to grow.

My relationship patterns were becoming clear to me, and I could see I had been doing what I think many women do, focusing so intently on proving that we're worthy of someone else's love that our own needs get lost in the process. I developed this pattern of performative love early in life; I can see it was present in my relationship with my father, where I felt on some level that if I could be a certain way, he would love me the way I wanted to be loved. In my early relationships, I thought (at least on a subconscious level) that if I checked all the perfect girlfriend boxes, then I would be rewarded with a happy, successful relationship. Rather than showing up authentically, I went all-in on catering to someone else's needs, and I got lost in the process. It took me getting honest with myself to realize that I was dimming my own light to make the other person feel more comfortable. I had this feeling that if my light shined too bright, I'd be too much. Real love doesn't require us to prove our worth, though. All it requires is that we show up as our true, authentic selves.

As women, many of us are natural nurturers and healers. Without a certain level of self-awareness, it's easy to fall into the habit of trying to heal, help, or fix the other person. However, that is not our role in a relationship. You can support someone for a certain period of time, but at some point you have to be real about whether the other person is where you need them to be, emotionally, physically, spiritually, or what not. You have to recognize that you can't be the one to change or fix them, especially if they're not willing to do that on their own. So many times we fall in love with someone's potential when we really have to look at what's present, what's in the here and now. And if they don't have the level of emotional maturity or availability you need them to have, even if the sex is mind-blowing, you likely have to be honest with yourself and move on, if you're looking for a life partner, that is.

So, despite the sadness I felt over the ending of another relationship, I felt empowered at stepping into myself. I was starting to get to a place where I was no longer okay with accepting whatever meager breadcrumbs came my way in a relationship. I could see that what I actually wanted, and deserved, was the whole damn bakery. I would repeat some of these patterns in my next relationship, but thankfully, I would move through them a lot more quickly.

2

IN THE FALL OF 2019, I found myself signing up for a 200-hour Yoga Teacher Training, a commitment that would bring me to Santa Cruz, California, each month. My teacher, who'd been guiding me on my yoga journey, was leading it, and I felt called to join her. Little did I know that the training would not only deepen my practice but also prepare me for a time of immense change and loss. In late September, my grandma, who was basically another mother to me, passed away. The grief stayed close as I continued my monthly trips, seeking grounding in every pose, in every breath.

By March 2020, I had graduated from YTT, feeling a renewed sense of purpose and a heart brimming with gratitude. I was ready to share my new gifts with those around me. A week later, the world changed. The pandemic locked us all in place, and my sense of freedom and connection turned inward. I was sharing a house with a unique blend of people: two couples, a baby, and a woman who'd quickly become someone near and dear to my soul. Funny how life throws you curveballs that turn into blessings. We got locked down together in this strange, mismatched household, and somewhere between late-night heart-to-hearts and walks outside, we became besties. We later left that house and moved in together, at some point we started calling each other "wifey," The one I can always count on, whether we were dancing around the living room with our cats or trying (and usually failing) to dress them up for the holidays. We don't live together anymore, but that bond hasn't changed. Some people in your life come and go, but wifey? That's for life.

The pandemic was a time of struggle and uncertainty for many, but if I'm being honest, I didn't mind it. I saw it as an opportunity to adapt, connect, and make the most of a weird situation. One of the most fulfilling things I did was start a virtual book club for young girls. Together, we dove into the pages of *The Confidence Code for Girls*. Each week, I assigned a chapter for the group to read, and we'd gather on Zoom for a discussion. These sessions weren't just about the book; they became a safe space for connection, growth, and sharing.

The girls, aged 11 to 15, brought such unique perspectives to the table. It was incredible to see how the book sparked confidence and self-reflection in them. Hearing how its lessons resonated with their lives warmed my heart. In a time when the world felt isolated and uncertain, this little online community reminded me of the power of connection and growth, even across screens. It's a memory I'll always treasure. It was a shining example of resilience and the bonds we can create, even in the most challenging circumstances.

In addition, I had the incredible opportunity to teach for a nonprofit organization called the Young Entrepreneurs Academy. My role there was more than just a teaching position. It was a mission to empower young girls with real-world entrepreneurial skills. I guided them step by step through the process of building their own business plans, from dreaming up ideas to crafting a solid strategy. The experience culminated in something truly inspiring: preparing them to pitch their businesses to actual investors, Shark Tank style. Watching their confidence grow as they stood up to share their vision was one of the most rewarding moments of my life. It wasn't just about the business skills they were learning; it was about showing them, through my own experience, that starting and running a successful business wasn't just a far-off dream. It was entirely possible. I became passionate about being their real-life example and their guide as they took their first steps toward realizing that their dreams were within reach.

Around this time, an acquaintance I'd met at the Summit of Greatness mentioned she was looking for a roommate in Tulum for December. Half-joking, I asked if she was serious. She was. Our conversation went a little bit like this:

Her: Come to Tulum
Me: Girl, don't play, I will come
Her: I'm not playing, come.

Without even second-guessing, not even 30 minutes later my flight was booked. Tulum was one of the few places open and thriving during COVID. I began splitting my time between my life back home and the warm, breezy freedom of Mexico. One month there, one month here. The thought of making Tulum my permanent base settled in, and I even decided to invest in an apartment.

Later on in 2021, I would be reminded that plans were fragile. My melanoma returned, showing signs that it had spread to a lymph node in my neck. Once again, I faced surgery and the stark reality that my time wasn't guaranteed. The experience shifted something fundamental in me. I began saying "yes" to life's invitations. No more waiting for "someday." The awareness of impermanence pushed me to embrace every adventure that called me. That may have been part of the reason I found myself living the van life for a part of the following year.

Jeremy and I had met through a mutual friend, the way we all wish to meet someone these days, outside of the app world. Our first conversation took place over the phone when we talked about books that inspired us. We continued to text and chat on the phone frequently after that. He told me all about his van life adventures and juice fasts. He even got me to do a juice fast at one point.

We finally met in person in San Diego a couple months later, close to my birthday in January. I had arrived early for a women's retreat and had some time to explore before the retreat began. We watched a sunset together on the beach, which felt cute and sweet. There was a playful energy between us. Although our interaction to that point had been limited to phone conversations, it felt like we'd known each other a long time. We were friendly with each other, but in my heart I could feel a deeper sense of connection. A vibe.

After the women's retreat, I decided to extend my trip. My inner dialog weighed whether to return to Chicago's cold winter to celebrate my birthday or remain in California's warm sunshine and risk spending my birthday alone. In the end, Jeremy and I met up to go on a hike and watch another sunset together. It was a perfect evening. We even spotted a few dolphins dancing through the water. Before we knew it, we were looking at the moon in the sky. We made our way back down the cliff, strolled through a nearby farmer's market, and then embraced in a hug that felt like honey for the soul. One of those goodbye hugs where neither person wanted to be the first to let go.

From there I returned home to Chicago, and we continued to casually text and talk on the phone regularly.

A few months later, right before I left on another trip to Tulum, I noticed a bump in my neck. A lump, if you will. It was quite visible to the naked eye. When I looked in the mirror, I kept hoping that I'd wake one morning to find it had gone away. Looking back, I can't help but wonder why I wasn't more concerned with it at the time. Had I thought that I'd slept funny and as a result had a lump sticking out of my neck? What in the actual fuck was I thinking? I reflect back to that time and kind of see myself behaving like an ostrich with my head in the sand. I left for Tulum without having it looked into.

After about 3 weeks, at the end of May, this lump, a rather unwelcome guest, didn't seem to be going anywhere. I returned from Tulum and showed it to my Mom. The color drained from her face.

"Rachel, how long has this been there?"

"I don't know, maybe a few weeks?"

"A FEW WEEKS?! WHY DIDN'T YOU SAY SOME-THING SOONER?"

"I was hoping it might go away on its own."

I had an upcoming skin check scheduled with my dermatologist, so I figured it could wait until then. When I met with her though, she too was less than thrilled that I had waited. She immediately referred me out to a general surgeon, who scheduled me for a PET scan. Lo and behold, it was indeed cancer, once again rearing its ugly head.

I remember reading the results in my medical portal, muttering the words "met-a-static melanoma" under my breath again and again. "Met-a-static melanoma." Say that 10 times fast, and you'll have yourself a tongue twister. "Okay, so, what now?" I thought to myself. The surgeon called to schedule the excision. I knew that once again I would be fully sedated and going under the knife, with my neck now slated to be sliced open. I felt numb in those moments, almost as if I couldn't feel. I didn't know what to feel.

Two years prior I'd been told that I was cured. This wasn't how things were supposed to go. I had read about people with chronic illness or diseases who have "aha" moments. Before they received their diagnosis, they hadn't been living fully, and they came to see their situation as the permission they needed to start living their best life. The thing was, though, I was already living my best life. I was happy, I had my own growing business, I was working out, I was eating healthy. What was I doing wrong?

A couple of days after surgery, my neck still tender and stitched, I found myself on a plane to Mexico with my mom. It wasn't exactly the most conventional post-op recovery plan, but I needed something more than rest. I needed answers. My mind was swirling with questions. Why did this happen? What was my body trying to tell me? Was there something deeper I needed to uncover?

The energy healing conference felt like a lifeline, a chance to explore what traditional medicine couldn't explain. I wanted to believe that there was more to healing than what I had been told. Maybe this trip would open a door to clarity, to something that would finally make sense of it all. I was searching, not just for physical relief, but for meaning, for purpose, for hope. Even in my uncertainty, I felt a spark of determination. If there's an answer out there, I'm going to find it.

During this time in Mexico, I crossed paths with a couple who asked me to take their photo. They ended up introducing me to someone who would become a dear friend. We connected on Instagram and, not long after, she invited me to come join her in Costa Rica. Even though I had never met her physically, there was something about traveling to a retreat later that year to sit in a mushroom ceremony with her that felt like an immediate yes to me.

When I got back from Mexico, my texts and calls with Jeremy continued. I shared with him about what I was going through. Knowing the tough time I was having, he invited me to join him in his van in Montana. I began looking at flights and found some reasonable options. Before I knew it, I had booked a ticket and was set to fly out in a couple weeks. I was both nervous and excited. I'd never stayed in a van before and didn't really know what to expect. We were also about to spend every waking moment together for five days. Without a toilet, without a shower. Was I crazy? Maybe, but hey, why not? It was nothing but pure joy and excitement when I saw his van pull up to pick me up at the airport. There was that home-y hug again. Of course, we went to the nearest juice bar to discuss our trip.

"What do you want to do?" he asked.

"I don't know, nature?" I replied.

We found a nearby state park, basically a pond right off the highway, but I didn't care. It was perfect. The sun was shining, and it was exactly what I needed in that moment. As I basked in the sunshine beside this little lake, I felt Jeremy's arm wrap around me. I felt safe and held in his embrace. It felt natural. Pretty soon I noticed myself getting hungry. The juice only held me over so far. We hit up a nearby grocery store and stocked up on lettuce, tomatoes, cucumbers, and jalapenos. Jeremy followed a primarily raw vegan diet, and I was along for the ride.

Together, we cut up the ingredients for the salad, and I tried to pretend I was full after a meal more suited to rabbits. It was a romantic evening though. We spent time stargazing and even saw a few shooting stars together. One thing led to another, and before I knew it we were kissing on the roof of his van. Deciding to take it a few steps further, we got ourselves to the inside of the van. His hand was about to make its way down the inside of my pants before I stopped him to ask, "Wait a minute, did you wash your hands? You were slicing a jalapeno an hour ago." He licked his fingers and assured me, "No more spice!"

I decided to trust him and allowed him to take the next step. The next thing I know, I feel a fiery sensation erupt from my genitalia. I encouraged him to lick it off. (That doesn't work.) He then said he wanted to feel it himself. Though I assured him he would not want to experience this sensation, he wanted to proceed. Well, I let him. The tip barely entered before he erupted himself, "HOT!" he yelled.

We both rolled off each other, reached our hands into the cooler, and began icing our genitals.

The moment was over.

What did I learn? Always trust your intuition.

Over the course of the three months that followed, we would spend a week out of each month living the van life together. Despite those hours of intense closeness, however, things didn't really seem to be moving forward. On our last road trip from Oregon to San Francisco, I finally broached the subject, asking, "What are we doing here? I want to be in a relationship with you. What are your thoughts?" His response was tough to hear, especially on top of all the uncertainty around my own health struggles. He essentially told me that he didn't see a future with me.

Jeremy and I stayed friends, talking on the phone from time to time, but moving on from him wasn't easy. I knew I deserved more than what he could offer, yet I couldn't shake the feeling that we could have had a future together. That future wasn't part of his world, though. Accepting that still left me wounded.

Life has a way of weaving together unexpected connections, guiding us toward the people and experiences we're meant to encounter. It creates a domino effect that leads us exactly where we're meant to be. One such path unfolded during my time in Mexico a few months prior, setting the stage for a journey that would take me somewhere entirely new. After my van life adventures had come to a close, it was time for that Costa Rica mushroom ceremony retreat with my internet friend. I set the intention that sitting in this ceremony would provide me with answers. I wanted to get to the root of why the cancer was manifesting in my body. I thought I'd come out of this experience with an "aha" moment. Instead, I found myself talking to and crying with some trees. It was beautiful but not exactly the answers I was looking for.

Costa Rica's allure didn't fade, and I extended my stay to explore solo. I had my own "Eat, Pray, Love" chapter, one experience flowing into the next. Each encounter was shaping my life in ways I couldn't yet understand. While standing in line at customs filling out an entry questionnaire, I met a man. We'll call him Alejandro. He was reading *Many Lives, Many Masters*. We struck up a conversation, and it made the time spent in line at customs fly by. It turned out he owned a surf school in Jaco, a potential stop along my solo itinerary. Before we knew it, we were up next to get our passports stamped. We waved goodbye and didn't exchange contact information. I figured I'd probably never see him again. Maybe it was one of those fleeting travel moments, a connection meant only for that instant, but then again, maybe not...

My first stop after my retreat ended up being Jaco. I thought I'd go for a surf lesson, so I checked into my hotel, dropped off my things, and went out for a beach walk. In the distance I saw a canopy set up for what looked like a surf school, so I approached it. As I made my way under the tent, I saw this dark, handsome man.

"Alejandro?"

"It's me, Rachel—from customs."

I think he may have been just as surprised as I was to actually cross paths again. I arranged for a lesson from one of his instructors, but the tide wasn't quite ready for a surf, so I had some time to spare. He invited me to join him on a walk and took me on a hike to "El Miro," an unfinished, abandoned building where you can view Jaco almost as though you're among the clouds. It was beautiful, and we sat there talking about anything and everything, from aliens to past lives. The conversation flowed effortlessly.

My surf lesson was hardly extraordinary. I'm pretty sure I wiped out on every wave, partly because I was nervous. I knew Alejandro was watching me and snapping photos from the shore.

We watched the sunset together after my surf lesson, and he kissed me on the beach. It was a breath-stealing kiss, the kind where you're left feeling light-headed in the best way.

Alejandro invited me to dinner, and I said yes. There was an easy chemistry between us and the conversation. We went out for sushi, and by the end of the meal, I found myself deciding whether or not to go back to his place. For a moment, I hesitated, the old instinct to protect, to overthink. Maybe part of it was that I was still carrying around the quiet ache of my recent breakup, my heart still tender in places I didn't fully realize. But then I thought, fuck it... "pura vida." So I went.

It was hot, messy, and exactly what I didn't know I'd been craving, a night of feeling alive, wanted, and delightfully undone.

When I got back to my hotel, maybe a part of me wasn't sure I'd hear from him again. So I took matters into my own hands and booked my Airbnb for the next leg of my trip. And then, the next day, he did text me, inviting me to join him at Manuel Antonio, a beautiful national park about an hour away. For a moment, I wondered if I should change my plans, if maybe I should stay. But I chose to keep going. I was still finding my own footing, trying not to place my raw feelings onto someone else. Sometimes I wonder what would have unfolded if I'd stayed. But in that moment, choosing myself felt like its own kind of healing.

From Jaco, I caught a shuttle to Monteverde. My Airbnb was perched on a steep cliff, and the hosts, a warm-hearted couple, kindly offered to drive me from the main part of town. We shared a meal together, language barriers and all, and they gave me a tour of their land. We walked the trail down to a waterfall; a hidden gem tucked into the wild green.

I spent a few days breathing in the misty air, then made my way to La Fortuna, where I reconnected with friends who'd become digital nomads. These friendships, my newfound love for solo travel, and the sense of freedom that came with each adventure reminded me that life could be as full and wide as I was willing to let it be.

I had begun the journey thinking I was seeking something outside myself. But as each experience unfolded, it was as though I was shedding layers, finding strength, and learning that my own company, my own courage, was enough. In each step, from yoga to Tulum, to Costa Rica's coasts and cliffs, I discovered that I had, all along, been traveling toward myself.

3

∞

MY SUN-SOAKED SOLO ADVENTURE to Costa Rica had been as healing as it was exhilarating. Though I was a little sad my trip was ending, I felt relaxed and content breathing in the night air as I chilled in the hot springs and chatted with two friends I had met up with at the tail end of my adventure. They were curious about where I was headed next. "What's in Chicago?" one of them asked. "Why aren't you coming with us to Miami?"

As much as I didn't want to head back, I was booked on a morning flight to Chicago, with a cancer infusion treatment scheduled the following afternoon. It was a necessary and inevitable return to my relentless battle against the disease that now lurked insistently at the edge of my reality. My friend, however, was not deterred by the seriousness of my health situation. "Fuck cancer treatment," she said. "Come join us in Miami. We've got a penthouse booked and we've got some incredible events lined up."

My mind quickly began calculating, trying to figure out if and how I could make that happen, trying to defend why I couldn't possibly throw caution to the wind. I hadn't ever done anything so spontaneous, let alone when the stakes were so high. Before I knew it though, I had responded, "Fuck it. You're right. Fuck cancer treatment. I'm going to Miami."

Later that night in my hotel room, I tried to figure out exactly how I could reroute my flight to Chicago to travel instead to Miami. It turns out, it wouldn't even involve a change fee, evidence to my mind that it was meant to be. I texted my mom to let her know, "Hey, I am not going to be coming back to Chicago. I need to move the date of treatment. I'm going to go to Miami to join my friends there."

My mom wasn't exactly thrilled when I texted her about my change in plans, but ultimately, she understood my need to take a break and urged me to reschedule with my oncologist. After a brief discussion with my doctor, he reluctantly agreed to delay my treatment by a week or two. "It wouldn't be my recommendation," he said, "but I can't stop you from making that choice if that's what you really want. Just know that I wouldn't personally advise it."

After speaking with him, I felt a mixture of relief and doubt. Was I being foolish and impulsive by taking my friend up on her invitation? Why had I jumped at the chance to postpone the treatment? There was a part of me that felt an intense need to break away from the harsh reality of cancer treatments. I had always believed in the body's power to heal itself, and I was influenced by inspirational figures like Joe Dispenza, who spoke of miraculous recoveries achieved through personal development and alternative healing. I wanted to believe that I could find healing in the natural world, away from the harshness of immunotherapy and surgery.

Was my decision motivated by fear, a desire to escape the enormity of my diagnosis? Absolutely. There was an internal battle raging within me. I had been trying to convince myself that

I could overcome this disease through natural means alone. I wrestled with the idea of rejecting conventional treatments and had experimented with various alternative practices. My time in Costa Rica, surrounded by nature and hot springs and engaged in practices like yoga and meditation, only intensified this internal struggle.

I had sat in a mushroom ceremony and engaged in a back and forth inner dialogue, trying to work through my internal battles. I remember thinking, "If I can just sit in this mushroom ceremony, maybe I can work through all of my trauma and figure out exactly why this is happening. Then maybe I can find a way to cure it and fix it. I will work through all of my past life trauma. I will work through all of this current life trauma, anything that has ever happened in my past, and this will be it."

It was the same with other plant medicine ceremonies that I had sat in, because again, I had heard that some people are able to cure themselves that way. I wanted to do everything that I could the natural way, and not have to rely on doctors and the hard treatments of modern medicine. The surgeries, the immunotherapy, the resultant rashes and other unpleasant side effects. I wanted to prove to myself that I could do things naturally.

My friend's enthusiastic suggestion, "Fuck cancer treatment," was a catalyst of sorts. It was the nudge I needed to give myself permission to explore an alternative path. The opportunity to immerse myself in Miami's conscious social scene felt like a chance to explore healing in a new and exciting way.

I decided to reroute my trip to Miami and soon found myself in a penthouse with a vibrant group of like-minded individuals. The events were alcohol-free, and I met some incredible people, all of whom were focused on genuine connections and personal growth. It was a deeply fulfilling and rejuvenating experience. As I hugged one of my new friends goodbye, she whispered in my ear, "Yes, life gets to be this fucking good." Her words resonated deeply in the moment, and they stayed with me afterwards, reinforcing my belief in the possibility of a life beyond not only the status quo, but beyond what I could imagine unfolding for myself.

I wanted to help as much as I could with making sure the penthouse events ran smoothly. I soon found myself and one other girl were put in charge of preparing food. That meant catering to about 80 people, something which I soon discovered was a really big job. We were trying to prepare an assortment of delicious, organic dishes when Nathan, who was in charge of taking video and photography at the event, came upon us furiously chopping vegetables in the kitchen. He saw that we looked overwhelmed and asked, "Hey, can I help you ladies with anything?" I immediately handed him a big bowl of kale and told him to "massage this kale."

Nathan and I became friends that night, talking at length as we worked alongside each other. There was a charged, flirtatious energy between us that provided a fantastic distraction, since I had spent a good portion of my time in Costa Rica trying to recover from my breakup with Jeremy. When I felt a spark between Nathan and me during my weekend in Miami, I was both intrigued and eager to see where it would lead. Our connection felt genuine and meaningful, and when he drove me to the airport at the end of the weekend, we promised to stay in touch.

When I returned to Chicago, I could no longer avoid the inevitable and showed up for the cancer infusion. The lightness I had experienced during my time in Costa Rica was interrupted by the weight of my diagnosis and everything that came along with it. I was determined to channel my energy towards something positive, though, so I shifted my focus into planning my 30th birthday.

I had originally planned to gather a handful of my closest friends and escape to the beach, but after my experience in Miami, I found my vision evolving into something much more expansive. I started to think of my birthday as a retreat, a celebration of connection and personal growth and an opportunity to forge deeper bonds and loving support. This wasn't just about marking another year of life; it was about cultivating an experience of gratitude for life. Yes, we would hang out together by the beach, but after what I'd experienced in Miami, I thought to myself, "What if I took it one step further? What if I made it a weekend of conscious connection?"

Once I decided I wanted to do that, I got excited. It was going to be my first time hosting a retreat experience, which was something I had always wanted to do. I felt I wanted someone to capture video and photos of this experience. I called Nathan, and he immediately said yes to the opportunity. When he was planning out his flight details, he asked me when I was getting there, and we both ended up planning to arrive a few days early to relax a little bit before getting into hosting and facilitation of the actual experience itself.

I had previously invited Jeremy to be part of the week-end, but his response was kind of one foot in, one foot out. Wanting to iron out the final details of accommodation for the weekend, I pressed him on his RSVP. The last thing he told me was, "No, I probably won't be able to swing it," so it was a bit of a shock when he showed up in the end, especially because Nathan and I had become intimate while spending several days alone together prior to everyone arriving. When everyone began arriving, and Jeremy stepped out of the last cab, I was instantly overcome with conflicting emotions. Excitement to see him, and panic over the fact that, "My god. Jeremy is here. And so is Nathan."

After greeting everyone with hugs, I pulled Nathan aside to quickly let him know that the guy I had been seeing, and who I had been navigating a heartbreak from, had just arrived. I explained that though Jeremy and I were no longer together, we remained friends. Nathan immediately nodded his head in understanding as he processed this information. His simple, yet reassuring, "Okay," made it clear that he was comfortable with the situation. He appeared to have a firm grasp on the complexities of past relationships and current connections overlapping.

I was relieved that the conversation went well, but I was distracted as I greeted my friends. I was thrilled by how excited everyone was to be together, but at the same time, I was mentally navigating the fact that I needed to tell Jeremy about what was going on with Nathan and me. When Jeremy eventually volunteered to drive a couple of my friends to the place they were staying, I decided to ride along with him.

When we pulled back into our villa, I plunged into the conversation, "Before we walk in there, I have to tell you something. As much as I'm really grateful that you're here, and am glad you decided to come, I think you should be aware of the fact that I have gotten together with Nathan in the days prior to you arriving." What followed was far more charged and emotionally intense than I had anticipated. He looked hurt and shocked, and his eyes brimmed with tears. He asked point-blank, "Did you sleep with him?" My simple affirmation that we had seemed to crush him. He buried his face in his hands and sobbed openly.

I felt guilty for causing his pain, but at the same time, I was confused. I sat back and asked, "What's going on? We're not together. You said you didn't want to be in a relationship with me?" He responded through his tears, "I know we're not together and you didn't do anything wrong, but it still hurts. It feels like a stab in the heart, one that I will have to work through on my own." Despite the emotional weight of the situation, I tried to hold space for him, offering compassion and understanding. We embraced, and I reassured him that while I recognized his pain, I also needed to stay true to my own choices and feelings.

The conversation was raw, honest, and real in a way that reflected both the complexity of human emotions and the messy intricacies of relationships. Navigating the conversations with these two men, and the emotions that came with them, was uncomfortable, but I knew that honesty was essential. If I was learning anything, it was that as much as we may not end up with a desired outcome in a relationship, staying true to ourselves is the most important thing.

They both stayed all weekend, and then Nathan stayed on for a week or two afterwards when my mom flew in. We continued our intimate encounter, but by the end of that time together, we both decided that we would be better off remaining friends. Neither of us was emotionally available for each other at the time, and I had learned enough about myself to know that, even though I wanted to be in a relationship, there was something missing. I just didn't feel like Nathan was "the one," the person I was meant to spend my life with. That being said, his role in my life was hugely important. He helped me cross the bridge of my heartbreak over Jeremy, the person who I had thought was "the one."

I had shown Jeremy unconditional love, and when he didn't offer me the same in return, it nearly broke me. I couldn't understand why he couldn't see a future with me. The appreciation and respect Nathan showed me during the time we spent together helped me see that I am enough, just exactly as I am, and whatever Jeremy thought was missing had everything to do with him and nothing to do with me. In that way, Nathan was a bridge, one that moved me closer to seeing the value of my authentic self. Because before you can find your King and settle down for your "happily ever after," you have to realize that you, yourself, are a Queen. I feel grateful that Nathan helped me to get there. He left Mexico with the promise that we'd stay in touch and that he would edit the videos and photos he took of the weekend.

When I reflected back on our conversations that weekend, I was able to see how true to myself I was, and how honest I was able to be with both Nathan and Jeremy. I didn't try to hold anything back or hide something from one and not tell the other. I presented each of them my truth to take as they wished, and then essentially invited them to move forward with having ourselves an amazing weekend.

The weekend retreat was everything I had hoped for and more. Each day was filled with intentional and magical experiences. From the first night when everyone arrived, there was a sense of excitement in the air. I encouraged everyone to rest, telling them I had planned full days ahead. Once everyone woke up on the first morning, we made breakfast together. Some people practiced yoga and meditated, and then we all gathered to set some intentions together. I asked the question, "What do we hope to get out of this weekend? Outside of celebrating my birthday, why are we here?" and we shared our responses. Though most of us knew each other already, that conversation brought us closer.

I wanted that night's party to be substance free, because so often we use alcohol as liquid courage and I just wanted people to connect authentically, to be themselves without inhibitions. I was so busy running around that day getting everything ready that I almost forgot to take a moment to pause and feel gratitude for everything I had arranged for the night ahead.

I had ordered a massive amount of juice and coconut water from my favorite local juice stand. I'd hired a few of my favorite DJs to perform, and decorated the villa with all kinds of vibey candles and lights. I had thought to myself, "This night is going to be perfect," and it was. Around 8 p.m. the guests began to arrive, and it filled my heart with joy to see every face that walked through that door. It felt like more than a celebration of another lap around the sun. It was an embodiment of my vision of deep connections, personal revelations, and shared experiences, and it left everyone involved feeling a deep sense of love.

I was overwhelmed with gratitude as I looked around at my friends. The gathering was a testament to the power of intentional connection and the strength of the community I had built. It was a milestone in my journey of healing and self-love, and it reminded me of the strength that comes from embracing life's challenges and choosing to surround yourself with supportive, kind, and loving humans. I made a speech that night, sharing a bit about my journey that year when I had undergone lymph node surgery. I told of being halfway through cancer treatment and the immense gratitude I had for being present with them, for being alive, for being on an earth journey alongside each of them.

The following morning I corralled my friends into doing a magical, lazy river float trip, one of my favorite activities to do when visiting Tulum where you get to explore the Muyil Mayan Ruins. As you make it past the ruins, you are greeted by a lush jungle which you hike through before it opens into the Sian Ka'an biosphere. It is a slice of heaven. A group of guides was waiting for our arrival, and we hopped into three separate canoes. Nathan, Jeremy, and I were together in one, and my friends filled two others. It was like a dream, meandering through the canals and watching these two men who I loved become friends with one another.

When it was time to put on our life jackets, we were instructed to step into the arm holes of the orange flotation devices with our legs, essentially wearing them like giant diapers. One by one, we jumped into the pristine cold waters and let ourselves be guided forward. At one point as we floated along, I decided to take off my bathing suit top, letting my girls be free. I kept my top off for a time after we got out of the water, just to feel the sun against my skin. I felt free and beautiful in my own skin.

We returned home to a pristine clean villa, which felt like a breath of fresh air after the party we had thrown. The private chefs arrived shortly afterwards, and soon the smell of seared steak filled the house. We all showered quickly to get ready for dinner. I had no idea what I wanted to wear, and found myself gazing at my naked body in the mirror, admiring the beautiful being staring back at me. I looked through the clothing options, and none of the particular outfit choices matched the energy I was feeling, so instead I chose to wear what made me feel most comfortable: a silky robe with a layered gold necklace. It was perfect. I felt at home in my own skin, light, unburdened, and completely myself. I descended the stairs and saw that many of my friends had already taken their seats at our round table.

I took my seat in between Nathan and Jeremy, in what felt like a dream. We were all starving, but before we could dig into our first course, I wanted each of us to share a word of gratitude. I asked them each to share a word they would use to describe me, and by the end, everyone at the table was in full blown tears. They were tears full of gratitude for the friendships we'd cultivated with one another and for the ride of life we were on together. As if that wasn't enough, I had met an angel of a human earlier that week, someone who had a voice of gold, and I'd hired him to sing and play guitar while we ate. By the end of dinner we were all dancing to the classic tunes of Eric Clapton and The Beatles.

But wait, there's more! I also had a couple of my close girlfriends come do a sound journey and energy healing session for all of us after dinner. Words cannot do justice to how magical the entire day was.

The decisions I made, to pause my treatment, to embrace spontaneity, and to honor my evolving needs, were all part of my larger journey towards personal empowerment and self-discovery as I navigated the messy, beautiful chaos of my existence. It was anything but neat and tidy, and it certainly wasn't easy, but there's something profoundly liberating about embracing chaos rather than trying to control or fix it. Each challenge and each heartbreak seemed to be leading me further into knowing myself and what it means to truly live. I was starting to see that it's not about making the perfect choices or finding the flawless path; it's about showing up with honesty, courage, and a willingness to evolve. Even when it felt like the universe was throwing plot twist after plot twist at me, I chose to confront my fears, lean into the discomfort, and honor my evolving needs.

Life will continually throw us curveballs, and we somehow need to figure out how to catch at least some of them. I was starting to see that authenticity isn't about having all my shit together or staying on a predetermined path; it's more about embracing all the ups and downs of life and trusting that each step, each choice, is leading us closer to who we are meant to become. Life's beauty often lies in its imperfections and in the courage we find within ourselves to handle it with a bit of grace. The path isn't always smooth or well-lit, but maybe it doesn't have to be.

These were good things for me to have realized, because three weeks later, I found out that I was pregnant.

4

OUR INTUITION never really screams at us. I was receiving these pings that I was pregnant earlier on the day that I found out. I was in a Marshall's dressing room trying on clothes, and while I was looking at myself through the fitting room mirror, I started puffing out my belly and then sucking it back in, puffing out my belly then sucking it in. I thought to myself, "Nah, Rachel, you're being crazy. No, there's no way you're pregnant. Stop it. Put your shirt back down."

I walked out of the dressing room and thought nothing more of it until later that same day, when I went in to have a CT scan. I came to the part of the pre-screening questionnaire where it asked the date of my last cycle. I wrote down that it had been 40 days, but that was still within the range of a normal cycle length for me. Still, it kind of made me think, "Hmmm, well, I am a little bit late." Then there was a question asking, "Do you think you could be pregnant?" and I just thought, "No. Wait... is there a chance?" When I handed the sheet of paper to the attendant, I just kept holding on to it. Then before he walked away I said, "You know what? Can I actually take a pregnancy test, please?"

I think I asked for the test more to rule out the possibility than anything else. I didn't fully think about what might happen. It was more like, "Let's just make sure we have all our bases covered. Let's just make sure that I'm actually not pregnant." This was my body talking to me. It wasn't my head. My head was saying, "No, you're not pregnant."

The CT scan was a follow-up from the surgery I'd had in June to remove the metastasis on my lymph node. This was the halfway point in my course of follow-up immunotherapy, essentially to see if the treatment was working, what they called the cleanup crew. I had been going in for monthly infusions and had gotten through seven rounds of that. Although it was more or less a routine check, I remember feeling this low-level frustration. I didn't want to have to be going through this.

I'd just come from a place of such a high with my 30th birthday celebrations, only to find myself back in the hospital. That was the reality of my life though. I got to have the amazing, conscious experiences I was having at the time, but then the alternate side of my reality was a little damper, darker, and not that much fun. More than anything I just wanted to have fun and live my best life and not have to worry about cancer treatment. At that point I was feeling pretty negative about conventional medicine and big pharma. I wanted to just sit in my meditation, sing Kumbaya, and have everything be okay.

I was also trying to share about my journey online so I could try and be an inspiration for others, sharing how grateful I was to be living my life, including this part of my experience where it was just really, really challenging.

I'd chronicled some of my journey on Instagram, posting stories and posts that would show the rashes and other side effects of immunotherapy treatment. I didn't get to just waltz into an office and get an IV drip and waltz back out. I'd be prescribed topical steroids to help subdue the rashes I would get, and I was tired a lot of the time, especially after the infusions, which I was actually highly allergic to. I had to be pre-medicated with an IV drip of Benadryl before starting the infusion itself. It was always a tough, lonely experience. Even though my mom was there, and my roommate at the time was incredibly supportive, it was still a very lonely experience, because at the end of the day, I was the one going through it.

After I peed in the little cup for the first test, the nurse went away for what felt like an eternity, although it was probably more like five minutes. Then she came back and said, "Let's check this again." I quickly asked, "What happened the first time?" And she said, "It came back... positive." I hopped out of my seat and said, "What? Positive? Are we sure? Did you read it correctly?" I was looking at the same test that she was looking at. Then I watched the second test process, watching first as one line showed up, and then shortly after a second line appeared showing it was positive. Two bright pink lines. There was another nurse in the area, and the nurse who was helping me said, "Let me ask my supervisor." Then they performed a third test, dipping the pipette once again into the cup holding my pee, and dropping it into the test. I'm not sure what we thought we were accomplishing by calling in the supervisor, other than a sense that we wanted some higher authority involved because we weren't sure we liked the outcome we were getting.

As all this was happening, I was just starting to process its magnitude in my mind. At one point I said, "I ate a lot of oranges today. Could that possibly be skewing the test somehow and producing a false positive?" as though that's where babies come from, from eating too many oranges. I sat there and started to shake, partially from cold (it was February and I was wearing a paper-thin hospital gown) and partially from the shock of receiving this new information. The attendant asked me, "Are you okay?" I said, "No, no, no, let me tell you a bit of my story." I started telling her how I was there for the CT scan, because I was currently undergoing cancer treatment, and that I don't want to be going through cancer treatment, but that's the reality of it. I am. I told her, "Also there was this guy that I really, really liked. His name's Jeremy, and I thought that there was a possibility him and I could work things out and be together and fly off into the sunset. But no, Jeremy decided that he didn't want that, and then I was intimate with another man, Nathan, who had done video and photo for my birthday party. Even though we were intimate, we ultimately decided to remain friends, and I am almost 99% certain that this is his child... and we're not, I don't know, this is not how this story goes. This is not the story that I had written. What am I supposed to do here?"

She paused and said, "Um, I'm here for you." I took a breath and asked, "So the CT scan is not being done today, right? So I'm free to go?" She nodded and asked if I was alright to drive. Soon after I found myself putting on my coat and getting behind the wheel. I dialed a number to call Nathan and let it ring as I was driving and shaking at the wheel. I think Nathan could hear the shakiness in my voice, and he told me, "I think you should pull over." I said, "Cool, there's a CVS. I'm going to pull over, and I'm going to buy another two pregnancy tests." Obviously the news that I was pregnant was a shock to both of us. In that moment, he was just there on the other end of the phone to hold space for me to breathe through taking it in. When I hung up the phone with Nathan, I actually called another one of my girlfriends and told her what was happening. She just kind of held space for me as well.

I came through the door of our house with a CVS bag holding two pregnancy tests and marched into my upstairs bathroom, where my mom greeted me and asked, "How did the CT scan go?" I was opening up the two boxes of tests and she asked, "What's in the bag?" so I told her, "I did not have the CT scan, Mom. The pregnancy test came back positive at the hospital and I have two more pregnancy tests here that I'm about to pee on, and I will let you know the outcome."

She tried to hide her excitement, saying, "Wow. This is great, but ultimately, this is your choice, so I will just, I will leave you to it," and she did. Shortly afterwards, my fourth pregnancy test of the day came back positive. This one didn't have two pink lines on it either. It just said 'pregnant.'

I was pregnant.

The thought went through my mind, "Well, I'm 30 years old. Maybe this isn't exactly what I thought was going to happen.

47

I thought I was going to do the whole traditional marriage thing and then have a baby, but who am I to go along the grain and do things the traditional way? Nothing in my life is traditional. In many ways I fly by the seat of my pants, like booking spontaneous trips and traveling solo, starting my own business and forging my own path instead of working a traditional 9-5." I thought to myself, "I'm 30. Why not? I can give this child a beautiful life." When I asked myself what I was going to do, whether I was going to go ahead even though this wasn't what I had planned, my mind and body and soul was a full "Fuck yes. This baby is choosing me. This baby was sent to me in Divine timing. This didn't happen by accident. And what a blessing it will turn out to be." I felt like the Universe was telling me, "Yes, absolutely. This is meant to be. This baby is choosing you."

I had a feeling come over me right then where I knew that this was coming to me for a reason, and there was no doubt in my mind about having the baby. It didn't matter to me whether Nathan would be an active participant in the baby's life or not. At that point I just felt, "This baby is a miracle blessing, and I receive it with full arms." In fact, I remember at one point, Nathan saying something like, "What happens if something happens to you?" I came right back with, "What if something happens to you? What if YOU get hit by a bus?" I felt like he was basically implying that I somehow had a death sentence hanging over my head because of my cancer diagnosis. At some level, it helped me see, essentially, that I wasn't going to live like that.

I couldn't and wouldn't live life in fear of something happening. I refused to let myself be at the effect or the mercy of my diagnosis. Instead, I was taking my power back and not letting that uncertainty cloud my entire life. Yes, it was a fact of life, but in the same way that it's a fact of life for anyone. Life is uncertain for all of us, and there was tremendous power in recognizing and voicing that. In a way it further cemented my feelings of certainty around the fact that yes, I was going to be a mother, and that it was incredible.

This was reinforced a few days later on a Friday morning, when I noticed that I was spotting. I started to get really scared, which to me was another piece of evidence showing me how much I wanted this, how much I wanted to be a mom. I knew that I wanted to have this baby. I called my gynecologist right away and arranged for a visit the following Monday, when my mom and my best friend came with me and I had an ultrasound. When we heard the heartbeat, I remember feeling like, "Wow. This is the craziest, most amazing sound in the entire world." I felt more than anything that I'd been blessed with a miracle, and I was so grateful for what was unfolding in my life.

After I found out, I had a meeting with my oncologist, who told me, "Obviously we're going to stop cancer treatment," and somewhere inside me I felt, "Yes, this is exactly what I was asking for, because I wanted to stop treatment. I did not want to do this anymore. Wow, God, universe, thank you. I'm done now." The oncologist even said to me, "Based on the rashes you were getting, I feel that your body was showing us that it was reacting to the immunotherapy." He said, "I feel comfortable saying that I think you've had sufficient treatment for us to pause at this point, and we'll scan you after the baby is born and determine where we go from there." Funnily enough, at that point I recalled how when I first started immunotherapy, they told me to use two different types of contraceptives, to double down on my birth control, just to be sure. Even though I had said, "Yes, I hear you..." I decided, on some level, that I was going to go off and do something else. It wasn't a deliberate rebellion, not really. So many of the choices we make happen in our subconscious, shaped by instincts, habits, or some quiet resistance we don't fully acknowledge. Maybe I had already decided, without realizing it, that I wanted to reclaim some sense of control over my body. Or maybe I just didn't want to believe that I needed that kind of precaution. It's not like I had a steady boyfriend. Plus, "pull and pray" had been working for me for 13 years.

On an even deeper level, this was something I had wanted all along. There was a part of me that had always longed for motherhood; it had been weaving its way through my subconscious and manifesting in ways I hadn't been fully aware of until now. When I was younger I dreamt about the day I'd become a mother. Then, when I found out about the pregnancy, I began dreaming in earnest about what kind of mother I'd be: raising my child in nature, traveling the world together, and building a life filled with adventure and wonder. But even as

49

those visions took shape, a question lingered in the back of my mind: could I really raise this baby on my own?

My mom raised me as a single mom, and we've always had a close relationship. I think in many ways she overcompensated and took on the role of "supermom," working long hours as a doctor while balancing being there for me. She juggled so much and yet still managed to show up as the most loving mom a girl could ask for. I think for the longest time I wasn't even willing to see her shortcomings because I was so focused on the fact that she had done so much for me.

Growing up with a single mom taught me strength and resilience, but it also wired me for hyper-independence. I learned early on that needing less from others meant less disappointment. I became the kind of person who prided myself on handling everything alone: strong, capable... "I got this." But the thing about hyper-independence is that it doesn't just protect you from pain; it also keeps you from connection. Real strength isn't about never needing anyone. It's about knowing when to let people in.

I found myself at a point in my life where I was turning inward. I was figuring out who I really was and what I was made of. In many ways, it wasn't about learning. It was about unlearning. Unlearning everything I thought I knew about strength. What it means to be seen. To let people in, specifically men. That was where it felt complicated.

My relationship with my mom had always been my safe place. Steady. Solid. She was the one who showed up, who stayed. But with my dad, things felt different. His presence came with distance, and eventually, absence. My parents divorced when I was five. He had been sober during their marriage, but after the split, he started drinking again. I still remember sitting beside my grandmother's deathbed at thirteen, when he told me he was an alcoholic. He framed it in a serious way but also with a strange nonchalance. He said he just drank more than most people but didn't really get drunk. But even then, I had a sense the truth was more complicated than what he'd so casually described.

When I was much younger, my dad had "forgotten" to come pick me up more than once. At the time, it was always framed as something else. He had a last-minute work meeting or an important business trip he couldn't miss. But as I got older, I began to see through the stories. He hadn't been working. He'd been on a bender. Drugs and alcohol were part of the equation, though no one had said it outright back then. What I understood, even as a kid, was the feeling: I wasn't a priority. And it hurt. That wound deepened when I learned he had cheated on my mom with our nanny. That betrayal lodged itself inside me in ways I wouldn't fully understand until much later. It became part of the quiet programming that shaped how I saw men, how I trusted, or didn't.

Growing up, it was hard to bond with him. He missed a lot. I taught myself how to ride a bike. Sometimes, when we were supposed to spend time together, he'd bring me to work and assign me math problems. I didn't mind, really. I got good at it, even ended up in honors math classes. But what I really wanted was presence. Attention. To feel like I mattered.

Then, when I was fifteen, he nearly died in a house fire. Three years later, he was diagnosed with lymphoma, and something in me softened. I forgave him for the ways he had fallen short. We started to rebuild, slowly, awkwardly, but genuinely. I'd visit him once a week. We'd play pool and talk about college life. We even took a trip to California together. And then, when I was twenty-one, he left this earth.

And somewhere along the way, I internalized the idea that men leave. That no matter how much love is there, it's not a matter of if, but when.

So I learned to protect myself. I kept men at arm's length. I got good at bonding with women. Those relationships felt natural, intuitive. I could be vulnerable there without fear of abandonment. But with men, it was always harder. I couldn't quite trust that they'd stay, so I didn't let them get too close.

Looking back, I can see how much of that was about self-preservation. It sprung directly from my emotional muscle memory. But at this point in my life, as everything became stripped down and raw, I started to wonder if maybe strength didn't mean shutting people out. Maybe it meant opening to love, to presence, to the possibility of being held.

51

And in a parallel way, I was receiving this sign from my body to be present. A missed period. The two pink lines on the pee stick. The clear sign from the universe that it was time to level up. To surrender and trust.

5

∞

IN SOME WAYS I felt like it was the answer to my prayers when I found out I was pregnant. There was a part of me that had been wanting to stop treatment, and I felt like my body was telling me the same thing as well. The rash caused by my immunotherapy infusions had made me feel uncomfortable in my own skin in so many ways. Then all of a sudden there was a very clear sign that, "Oh, I can no longer continue treatment." From there I was able to focus on just nourishing my body and feeling good about everything that was going inside of it. It was like I suddenly regained my power of choice, and that everything that would go into my body would be of my own choosing.

Even though I knew I had been taking care of myself when I chose to do immunotherapy, what I really wanted was to treat myself holistically. By suddenly receiving the blessing of being pregnant and carrying a being inside of me, I was able to really nourish myself, take care of my body through yoga, work out, and do everything that I could to nourish myself and the baby that was growing inside of me. I really made it a priority to take care of myself by putting into my body what it was craving. In the very beginning of my pregnancy, I was craving oranges, so I took that to mean that I really needed vitamin C. I didn't have any really crazy cravings outside of wanting to eat five or six big, juicy navel oranges in one day.

What was amazing was the feeling that I was making these choices from a space of me, rather than the space of what doctors were telling me to do. I had shifted to a place of asking what do I truly desire for myself in this moment. That's where I came from, not only with my food intake and working out, but also my desire to travel. During my pregnancy I was traveling almost every month to places that I knew would bring me joy, not just on a physical level, but also on an emotional and mental level. I went to places that make me happy to be in, Costa Rica and Colorado, but where I was also able to surround myself with the people I loved. I also got to spend time outside, connecting with nature, where I feel the deepest connection to the oneness that we all are, and the space of consciousness that we all are.

You know, we're here, connected to this Earth. We've been gifted this beautiful world that holds so much allure and magic, and she just wants to gift to us. I just wanted to connect with myself, connect with my future baby, Julian, and tell him about all the things we were getting to see together. I would just sit and hold my belly as he was growing and let him know about everything that I was seeing. I would sit by the ocean and hold my hands over my belly, and speak to him, "Hey babe, we're looking at the ocean right now. The waves are coming, and then the waves recede, and it's really beautiful. There's going to be a sunset soon. We're seeing some blues and some purples in the sunset," or, "It's raining outside right now, so we're sitting inside for a bit." I would constantly talk to him and connect with him that way while we were one, knowing that we were soon going to become two.

I felt a deep connection with the baby, and in a way I wanted to just be with him in what felt like our own little world. I wanted to form special memories of that time that I would cherish forever. When I reflect back on my pregnancy now, I get to see what a positive experience it was. I'm super grateful for that because I know it's not like that for a lot of moms, ones who deal with a lot of nausea and fatigue. I dealt with some of that, but I feel like I really got to capitalize on the times where I felt really great. There was this feeling of really knowing that this is what I was meant to do, to be a mom, even if the circumstances didn't unfold the way I'd always imagined they would.

I'd always thought that there would be a certain order of things: meeting a partner, getting married, buying a house, maybe getting a dog, and then having a child. But, at the end of the day, nothing in my life was ordinary, so it shouldn't have come as a surprise that my pregnancy was any different. Getting pregnant was obviously a surprise, especially while I was undergoing cancer treatment, but at the end of the day, I knew this was God's plan or the Universe's plan for me. When I found out I was pregnant, I was 30 years old, and thought to myself, "Now is as good as any time" to have a baby. If it had happened when I was a teenager, or in my twenties, I may have looked at it differently, but having embarked on my 30s, I knew it was sent to me for a reason.

I knew things would be a lot different after the baby was born, so while I was pregnant, I wanted to really embrace the energy of fun, and I knew I wanted to travel. I already had a trip on the books because the previous December, when I was still together with Jeremy, we had made a plan to go to a concert in Colorado. Finding out I was pregnant obviously changed my perspective on traveling with him, so I decided to invite two of my girlfriends to come with me instead. We hit the road together, and when we arrived in Colorado, met up with some friends I have who live there.

I was 13 weeks pregnant at that point, and as part of my prenatal care I did some genetic testing and had submitted a blood test about a week before I left on the trip. I had a feeling I would get the gender test results when I was there, and I think that's where I got the idea to do something a little different for my gender reveal. They called the day I arrived in Colorado, and when I saw the phone number light up across my screen, I picked up the phone, listened to them say they had my test results, and I explained how I wanted the gender to be a surprise. I handed the phone to my girlfriend and then afterward had her order cupcakes from a nearby bakery. I just had to hold on and wait to see whether they were filled with blue or pink frosting.

Cupcakes in hand, we hiked up to a mountaintop together. I had really wanted to include my Mom in the celebration. We tried a Zoom call and then Facetime, but there was barely any reception on this mountaintop. We had ordered her a tiny cake from a bakery near her home in Chicago, so we called her and put her on speakerphone while we bit into our cupcakes and she opened her cake box. We screamed in unison, her in Chicago and me with my friends on a Colorado mountaintop. I was going to have a boy!

I wasn't yet living with my mom at this point, but I think that was when she decided to start remodeling the whole house in anticipation of her new grandson's arrival. Back in Colorado my friends and I headed to see Rising Appalachia and Trevor Hall at Red Rocks. I didn't know who was opening the concert, and was beyond delighted when Gone, Gone, Beyond came out as the first opener. I started jumping up and down. I'd been listening to them the entire previous year, and absolutely loved them.

Red Rocks is the absolute most magical venue in all of the states. The sound is amazing. You're surrounded by these red rocks, and the combination of the acoustics and the music, along with just being outside is just so magical and special. All three of the artists performing have been very healing for me to listen to and I love the way that they convey their message. I love Trevor Hall's voice, and he's also a dad, so it was really sweet to see him and listen to him talk about the joys of being a father. It was an amazing night, just being able to be so present with the healing nature of music, getting to hug my friends and just to dance with them. It wasn't at all the concert I had originally anticipated when I planned it with Jeremy, but it ended up being the experience that I needed.

I also wanted to spend some time traveling solo while I was pregnant, which was part of how I found myself on my way to Costa Rica for prenatal yoga teacher training at 20 weeks pregnant. I was excited to be headed back there, and also looking forward to completing another thing I'd really wanted to do for a while. I had finished up my 200-hour yoga teacher training in March of 2020, and though I'd been curious about prenatal yoga, I had never really pursued it. There wasn't anything compelling me to do so. That changed once I was pregnant, because not only did it seem like something I wanted to learn more about for myself, but I also wanted to connect with my baby in this way. I also wanted to be able to help other moms through their pregnancies, and to help them with postnatal care, because often once our babies are born, our bodies are just not the same. Yoga helps us take care of our bodies and feel more connected to our bodies. It also helps with postpartum depression and anxiety.

I found a woman in Costa Rica who was leading a prenatal yoga teacher training which ended up being a one-on-one training. As well, I was able to stay next door to where she taught on a permaculture farm, run by a family who essentially lived off of their land. They grew everything on their own land, which was fascinating to learn about, because that's always been a dream of mine, to live off my land. They nourished me in so many ways. I would eat with them, learn about their culture and background, and then I would practice yoga. I had my lessons in the mornings and in the afternoons I had a lot of time for self-reflection, and for really being comfortable with being by myself, with myself.

I had originally anticipated being solo for most of my trip, but sometimes during my travels I would meet people and at one point I somehow ended up having a person tagging along with me. Out of a people-pleasing space, I said yes, and then spent several days with them under my wing until I realized that I actually didn't want to be traveling with this person anymore. As uncomfortable as it was, I had to speak up and tell them, "Hey, this is not working for me anymore. This is a trip for me to spend with myself and the baby in my belly, and I would like to part ways civilly." We ended up parting ways, and then when I got to my yoga teacher training the week after, I was able to unplug from the world outside of my training, and just spend

57

time with myself. It was a beautiful time in my life, and I was very grateful to get to be able to explore the nature of Costa Rica.

I knew I wanted to give birth naturally, so I went through a midwives group and also hired a doula. My Mom and I participated in an online birthing class together. Everyone else showed up with a husband or life partner, and there was me with my Mom learning about the Bradley method that included different types of breathing and positions to support you through a natural labor. It felt a little awkward at times, like we were out of place in a room designed for couples, but I also couldn't help but laugh at the situation. If anything, it made me even more grateful to have her by my side. I read Ina May Gaskin's *Guide to Childbirth*, and found it very inspiring to hear other birth stories. It gave me the confidence to know that this is what our bodies are made to do, that, yes, you can do it. My doula was amazing. She had been to our house a couple times prior to make sure that I was ready, although I don't know if any woman is necessarily completely ready, because every birth experience is different. Just like anything in life that is worth doing though, we can't really ever say we're really 100% ready. We just have to take that leap of faith, and that was me as I "got ready" for labor.

I had a nesting phase where I found myself getting things ready for the baby, including completely rearranging our Tupperware cabinet one night when I was 38 weeks pregnant. That was when I went into labor, while catching up with a really close friend named Drake. We were FaceTiming, and he said something that made me laugh. All of a sudden, I told him, "Drake, either my water just broke, or you literally made me pee myself. I'm bringing you to the bathroom with me to check." I pulled down my underwear, giving him the play-by-play: "Yeah… there's no way I just peed. I think I have to let you go and tell my mom my water just broke."

Wet underwear around my ankles, I waddled in to tell my mom, "I think my water just broke." Then, when I went to change into something dry, a second whoosh of water came out of me. There was no question at that point that my water had broken. My mom started pacing around the house getting things ready, and thankfully we already had our hospital bag packed. I messaged my doula, and texted my best friend to tell her, "Hey, it's happening!" but it wasn't until about two hours later that my contractions started. At first they were very irregular, happening every once in a while, almost like light cramps that came every 10 or 20 minutes, and then they started to increase in frequency, so I started my contraction timer.

At this point, my mom is ready to roll and I am here trying to explain to her that my doula was telling me to, "Go take a shower and get some rest." My mom, on the other hand, was saying, "Rachel, we need to go to the hospital. I don't want you giving birth to this baby in our house or on the highway." I was using a contraction timer app that could be shared with multiple people, so I'd shared it with my mom and my doula. My mom said, "Rachel your contractions are every five minutes. We need to go right now!" At that point, it was around midnight or so that we got in the car and headed to the hospital. Thankfully we seemed to hit every single green light on our way to the hospital, because my contractions started getting more intense and I was really feeling things. We pulled up to where it said emergency and were pointed in the right direction to get signed in for triage and then they measured to see if I was dilated and checked me right into labor and delivery.

My doula arrived about half an hour later and my soul sista best friend, Doris, arrived about a half hour after that. Things were becoming very intense. I'd made it through my entire pregnancy without throwing up but there I was, in labor and puking into the hospital barf bag. Thankfully, I had electrolytes in one giant water bottle and plain water in another and was drinking back and forth between the two. My doula kept reminding me to breathe. Though I'd been practicing breath work for a very long time, this was a whole other level of breathing.

I'm taking drinks of my electrolytes and my water, my doula is recommending laying on my side with a peanut ball between my legs, and then I remember my soul sista best friend Doris, walking in and I just saw her in this shining light. I said hello and immediately threw up into a barf bag, and continued on with the ceremony of birthing my son.

Not only was I vomiting, but things were coming out the other end too. It was anything but glamorous. I tried to relax, shifting positions in search of comfort, but nothing felt right.

Eventually, I accepted the inevitable. I had a new companion for the night: the toilet. I kept getting up, only to return, straddling it, resting my head against the tank, as if it were both my partner and my best friend, guiding me through this intense process.

Sitting on the toilet helped really move the baby down and loosen my hips. Meanwhile, my doula and my mom helped with double hip squeezes to alleviate some of the pressure my extremities were experiencing.

After some hours of this intense labor, I was moving around and suddenly felt the intense need to poop again, so I ran to the toilet to try and relieve myself. The nurse rushed in and said, "This is not a time to try and poop, it's time for you to start pushing!" so I crawled back onto the hospital bed, got up on all fours and started pushing the baby down.

To alleviate the pressure of the pushing I was squeezing a comb in my left hand, and I heard them telling me, "We can see the head beginning to crown." They asked me if I wanted to touch it and though I thought to myself, "Not really. I just want to see him, I'll feel him soon enough," I did try reaching around but couldn't reach him. I really just wanted to focus on the moment and on getting him out of my body. Eventually, I felt an intense release and alleviation of pressure, and I heard the words, "He's here," so I turned over and laid down, and they handed me my son for the very first time.

He was still attached to me by the umbilical cord. I birthed the placenta shortly afterwards. I just laid there holding him close to my chest. Then I saw him, looked into his eyes and saw him for the first time, thinking, "Just look at you. You're here." There he was, so beautiful, his eyes open and I think at this point I could really only see his black, dilated pupils. I probably appeared to him as a mixture of blur and color. I can imagine if he had any sort of thoughts, they were, "What is this crazy world outside of my mom's belly?" As you can imagine it would have felt really cold for him being outside of me all of a sudden and he started crying a little bit. I just comforted him, "Mommy's right here I got you," and he wrapped his little tiny fingers around my index finger. I just held him and looked at him, saying, "You just hold on to me, Mommy's got you," and I was filled with gratitude.

They told me it was time for me to cut his umbilical cord, but I said I wanted to wait at least five minutes until all of the blood flowed into him, and after that they handed me the scissors and I cut the cord. It was such an empowering, feminine moment for me, one that was deeply symbolic as well. Cutting the cord that connected us took us from where we essentially were one, to where we were two separate beings, and he was beginning his own journey outside of my body. It was day one for him: October 7, 2022.

After some time of holding him chest to chest, they took him away to weigh him and get his vitals. After what felt like an eternity, they returned him to me and my doula helped me to pump the colostrum out of my breasts. I latched him on for the first time, and I began to feed him, which was not only a new learning for both myself and him, but just such a beautiful experience. I am so grateful that throughout that entire process, I had my mom, my doula, my soul sista best friend right there by my side. The three of them held space for me as I moved through the ceremony of birthing life into this world.

The following day I sent a message to Nathan saying Julian was "officially earth side!" along with a photo of him swaddled in that pink and blue striped hospital blanket. I can't remember exactly what he said in reply, but what I do remember was it took him a full day to respond about his son being born.

SIDEBAR: In case I don't circle back later, Nathan is a loving father to Julian. We're friends now, raising him with warmth and respect. In the enormity of the birth experience, that felt like a mere blip in the background, however. I was more focused on the magnitude of what I'd just gone through.

I'd made the choice to have a natural birth because I wanted to feel all of it. It's something my body, our bodies, are meant to do. Yes, it was intense. At one point I wasn't sure if I would be able to do it. I was in such intense pain that I looked my doula dead in the eye and said, "I can't do it. I can't. I'm done. This hurts. I don't want to do it anymore." She just replied, "You're halfway there." I countered, "I can't do it." And she just said, "Yes, you can, you can, you can." I remember looking at her again, nodding in agreement, and thinking, "You're right, I can, I got this. I can, I can, I can." My mom told me, "The drugs

61

are there for you if you want an epidural right now, it's there for you," but I shook my head and said, "No, I got this. I will do this," and I carried on.

I think my whole labor only consisted of two or three hours of deeply intense contractions. It started around 8pm, we got to the hospital around midnight, and then at two in the morning, I thought, "No. Tap me out coach. Tap someone else in." I had this feeling of "Am I allowed to give up?" And it's like, no, you can't. You're in your body. Your body is having this process. You have to birth this baby. And by 6:56am the little man was earth side. At every moment I felt so connected with my body. Did I believe at every moment that I could do it? No, I think I had doubts, but it's one of those things where you're on a journey and you know there is some sort of destination, the birthing of your child, but you can't see the path to get there. You just have to trust in the process that, yes, your body is going to do whatever it needs to do. I am very grateful that my birth was relatively short with me only actively pushing for the final hour. And I found this newfound respect for every single mother out there.

During those hours though, I went through every spectrum of emotion. I felt the ecstatic joy and happiness of being handed my child for the first time. I'm not sure that's the way every new mother feels when they are handed their child, but I definitely felt in awe. It felt like a miracle to have this beautiful baby in front of me that grew inside me over the course of nine months. I also felt fear, doubt, anger, frustration, and maybe even sadness at some points, but I just went through it all, moving towards this place of new life, and also the reverse, where I was leaving behind or releasing whatever was. I had been one, and then I created something that is now two. It was a process of coming home to myself.

In the time that followed Julian's birth I felt the hormones shift in my body, and though I didn't experience full-on postpartum depression, I did go through an initial stage of feeling a little blue. Everything was making me cry, and I could hardly hold a conversation in those first couple weeks. I had to stay in the hospital a couple of extra nights because Julian was jaundiced, so they had to place him in a little bed under blue light.

It was hard to see him lying there completely naked looking so cold when I just wanted to hold him close and keep him safe. They even put him into the box incubator under the lights. Even though they had assured me that this was common, it was still so hard to watch, when all I wanted was to be home, starting our new lives together. I was grateful they didn't have to take him away from me entirely. On the bright side, I was producing breast milk to be able to feed him, and during that extra time in the hospital, I was able to call the lactation experts and really settle into a groove of feeling comfortable and confident with breastfeeding.

I'd created a new life, and I had to focus 100% on making sure that this new life continued living. I had to take care of him. I know I'm not alone in this. I've heard many other mothers talk about tiptoeing over in the dark to where their newborn is sleeping and putting your finger under their nose to make sure that they're still breathing. It felt entirely natural, and entirely new at the same time. I'd spent so many years living a life that was mine alone, and now that had all changed. It was no longer me alone. It was me and Julian.

6

∞

I WAS ENJOYING being in the little bubble along with my newborn baby, and was solely focused on trying to navigate all the things that come along with that. Like any mother, I was intently focused on my baby. He was my whole existence for a time, and I felt very protective of him. That was challenged when his father came to meet him about a month after he was born and brought along the person who, at the time, he called his "Divine life partner." I could sense that Nathan wanted us to be friendly with each other, but every cell of my being wanted to keep her away from my son. I remember thinking that her energy felt like blech, almost slithery, and I didn't even want to allow her into this space with me and my child, let alone have her taking pictures of him and being right in his face. I resented the intrusion and was relieved when they left. It meant I could return to enjoying my baby-moon space with Julian. Unfortunately that contentment was short-lived, though, because the universe had other things in store for me.

All three of us, Julian, my mom and myself, got COVID in December and then I started getting terrible headaches on a consistent basis. I tried IV infusions to see if they would help and then I thought that maybe acupuncture would do the trick. I just couldn't figure out what was going on. Was I holding a lot of stress or tension postpartum? Was it the lack of sleep? The headaches would come in what were almost rolling waves, where my head would throb for a period of maybe five minutes and then subside or go away. I didn't always feel like Tylenol or Ibuprofen was necessary, so I would ride the wave of each horrible migraine, feeling the pain, and then I'd be okay. After a while though, they started to get more aggressive and more frequent.

I had a midwife visit scheduled for my six-week postpartum checkup, but it kept getting pushed out for one reason or another. When my midwife appointment finally happened in January, I told her, "Hey, I've been getting these pretty frequent headaches. Do you think I should touch base with my oncologist about this?" She said, "Yeah, it's probably a good idea."

By the end of January I connected with him and let him know, "I'm having these really frequent headaches. I wanted to let you know about them, to see if there's anything we should do. My midwife says it's probably postpartum... and I'm hoping that that's the case." He agreed and said it was likely something postpartum, or from lack of sleep, but said, "Let's get you in for an MRI, just in case."

The MRI was scheduled for February 6, and the following day I received an alert on my phone that my test results were ready to view. This was at 6:30 in the morning, and I was kind of still waking up. I remember scanning through all the medical jargon, and then my eyes landed on the words, "lesion resembles metastatic melanoma to the brain."

I thought to myself, "My brain. This is my brain. We're not talking about some skin lesion you can cut out. This is my brain." In that moment, I felt somewhat numb, but also frantic at the same time. It was surreal really, because this was all happening as I gazed into my son's bassinet where he slept, soundly, sweetly, and unaware of my growing panic. I ran into my mom's room, desperately needing comforting. I needed to feel like it would all be okay. I immediately opened my web browser to see when my doctor's office opened, not for another two hours, and every passing minute that I had to sit with this news without knowing what would happen next felt like an eternity. I tried to digest what this would mean for my life. My son was only four months old, and I was just beginning to navigate what it meant to be a new mother. This was not what I thought this year was going to look like. This was not the life I had signed up for. I thought all of the bad stuff was behind me.

I felt so many emotions, panic, disbelief, anger, and they all crystallized into the question, *"What in the actual fuck?"*

Just a month prior, I'd been sitting quietly nursing Julian in a state of ecstatic joy, thinking to myself, "Wow, life is so beautiful." I was just so happy to be in the position I was in, in that simple moment, sitting in my white rocking chair with my son, just rocking back and forth. I'd felt so connected with him, nourishing him with my own body, and I thought that was what the upcoming year was going to look like. To be presented with this news completely shook me to my core. I thought to myself, this just isn't fair. I didn't exactly slip into a victim mindset, but I certainly found myself questioning, why is this happening?

I truly believe in trusting in the universe and having gratitude for its divine plan, but to be handed this news was almost too much. I'd already navigated through such a massive storm, the torrential downpour of skin cancer, the hail of an unexpected pregnancy, only to be greeted with an avalanche that felt like it would bury me from head to toe. I thought I would at least have a chance to rest on the mountaintop and enjoy the view for a little bit.

What I've come to see though, is that I will always find a way to weather the storm, that I have what it takes to find my inner strength time and time again. It's about finding the light and coming back to it over and over and over again. It's knowing that there is a light, and that the sun will always shine again. That like nature, storms will always come, but true resilience is about continuing to trudge ahead, even if we're not equipped with all the gear we might need.

When I finally spoke with Dr. Richards later that morning, he helped to calm me down and made me feel like there was a plan in place to handle what was happening. I wanted to see him right away, so my mom and I went into his office, and right then and there he walked downstairs with us to the neurosurgeon's office. He explained what the plan was going to be. I would be scheduled for brain surgery.

Of course, I peppered the neurosurgeon with questions. What are the risks? What are the expected outcomes? Our brain controls literally everything, everything, but I asked about what was controlled by the specific part of my brain where the lesion was. He suggested that I may have already noticed some changes in my vision in the area where the tumor had essentially taken over, and he did a peripheral vision test for me. It showed my vision on the right side in comparison to my left, and that delivered another shocking blow. Tears began to well up in my eyes as I uttered the words, "I can't see that anymore."

Before I even had a moment to process any of this, the neurosurgeon walked out of the office and in walked the scheduler. I'd be scheduled for brain surgery on February 17, in just 10 days. Let the countdown begin.

SIDEBAR: at home I'd begun noticing a decline in my cat's health. I had adopted him from an animal shelter back in college, along with two of my roommates. When one of the roommates was out of town, me and my soul sista best friend visited our nearest shelter and adopted him. We called him Bruce Lee and he was our little ninja kitty. He brought us so many snuggles and love. He loved to lay across our laptops when we'd be trying to finish our college papers. We loved to dance with him in the kitchen. He brought us comfort whenever we needed it. Upon finding out my own health news, I took my cat to the vet to run some blood tests and check on him. The following day the vet called to let me know that the blood test came back positive for feline coronavirus, which is typically fatal in cats. You have got to be kidding me, I thought to myself. The vet prescribed antibiotics and steroids, and I tried to administer them, but at this point he had already stopped eating and seemed to be shutting down. I was forced to accept the reality that I'd have to put him down. My best friend had come over that week to offer me support and comfort, so we were able to say goodbye to our beloved Bruce together. On February 15th Bruce was laid to rest, two days before I was to have brain surgery. Was this some sick joke? How was this real life?

The week leading up to my surgery was a blur of appointments, blood draws, and tightly scheduled consultations. Every day brought a new doctor, a new test, another set of reminders about "the plan." First the craniotomy. Then stereotactic radiation to a few other spots in my brain. Then immunotherapy. I nodded along, present in body but often far away in mind, because while they talked about tumors and treatment cycles, I kept thinking about something else: motherhood.

No one brought it up. I had to be the one to ask.

At first it was a whisper in the back of my mind: Will I have to stop breastfeeding? But soon it was all I could think about. I asked every doctor I saw, each time hoping the answer might change. Could I keep nursing? Would it be safe? Would it be before surgery or after? Before the radiation? Before immunotherapy? Was there any possible way to keep this part of my life intact?

I already knew the answer. But I kept asking anyway.

Breastfeeding wasn't just about nourishment. It wasn't just routine. It was sacred. It was the way I grounded myself when the world was spinning. The way Julian and I spoke to each other in silence. When everything else felt uncertain, this was something I could still do for him. With him. It was the thread that tethered us together in the dark.

And now I was being told I'd have to let it go.

I tried to make sense of it logically. I told myself, Of course it's not safe. Your body is about to become a battleground for medicine. But that didn't make it hurt any less. It didn't make it fair. I wasn't ready. This connection between us, it felt too beautiful, too pure, too essential to be yanked away from me by a clinical timeline.

Letting go wasn't just about the milk. It was about surrendering to a version of motherhood I hadn't imagined, one where I couldn't offer everything I wanted to. One where my healing would have to come first. I kept trying to rationalize it and feel gratitude for the 5 months of breast milk I did get to provide for him, but in that moment it didn't matter. There was no justification.

Breastfeeding was one of the purest, most profound bonds I had ever known. Those late nights and early mornings, when the world was quiet and it was just the two of us, his warm body curled into mine, his tiny hand resting on my chest, his eyes fluttering closed as he drank, it was more than connection.

I had grown him inside of me. And now I was feeding him from my body. I remember thinking how miraculous that was, how the same body that carried him, through everything, was still sustaining him. Still showing up.

It hadn't always been easy. In the beginning, there were tears. The frustration of learning how to latch. The frozen cabbage leaves tucked into my bra. The hot compresses, the throbbing pain of clogged ducts. But we had figured it out together, like a dance. We had built this rhythm that became our own language. And just when it started to feel natural, just when we had hit our stride, I had to stop.

It broke my heart.

I tried to focus on gratitude. Five months of feeding him from my body. Five months of nourishment, of closeness, of presence. I told myself that was enough. That I was lucky. That many don't get that much time. But still, it wasn't the plan.

In my mind, I had seen us going longer. A year, maybe two. I had imagined letting him wean when he was ready, not when I was told I had no choice.

Because that's what it felt like: that the choice had been taken from me. That something so sacred had been ripped away in the name of survival. And even though I understood it intellectually, even though I knew it was the right call for my health, it still felt like a loss I hadn't prepared for.

No one really tells you what it's like to say goodbye to breastfeeding. Not because you or your baby are done, but because your body, the same one that gave life, is suddenly under siege. Your body is about to become a vessel for surgery, radiation, medicine. No one can prepare you for the fact that to stay alive, you will have to let go of something that made you feel so incredibly and intensely alive.

I held Julian close that last night, letting him feed as long as he wanted. First on one breast, then the other. I memorized the weight of him, the sound of his breath, the feeling of his lips on my skin. I tried not to cry, but the tears came anyway. Not out of fear, out of grief.

And as he drifted off to sleep, full and warm in my arms, I whispered to him what I needed to hear for myself: This isn't the end. Just a new beginning.

7

∞

"HI, I'M NANCY," came a woman's voice sitting on my left.

"Hi, I'm Rachel," I replied.

Most of the people in that room were likely 40, even 50 years older than me, many of them hooked up to oxygen tanks, their bodies weathered by time in ways mine had been forced into overnight. I stuck out like a sore thumb. I remember everyone's looks as I stepped into the room for the first time.

I felt like the new kid in a school I didn't want to be in. I didn't belong here. I wasn't supposed to be here. But then these two women, Nancy and Sally, made me feel welcome in a place that none of us wanted to be in. They made space for me and made me feel a little less lonely.

Now, how'd I get here?

April 28th, 2023. Sayulita. The afternoon sun turned the pool into a sheet of shimmering light. Julian, seven months old, kicked his legs in his floatie, squealing with delight. I laughed, my mom and I sitting a few feet away from each other with our legs submerged in the water as we pushed him back and forth. Feeling the warmth of the water, the weightlessness of him in my hands. There was something about that moment, a stillness, a fullness, that made me think, This is it. This is happiness.

Then, blackness. A split-second void. And then—nothing.

I would only know later what happened next. How I convulsed, how my mother pushed Julian aside, how she reached for me, grabbed the ponytail of my hair, dragged me from the water. How she screamed for help, her hands shaking as she tried to turn me over, to clear my airway. How I came to for a moment, then slipped under again. How the ambulance rocked beneath me as I aspirated on my lunch. How a pulmonologist, in trying to clear my lungs, accidentally punctured one instead, resulting in a chest tube. How a ventilator took over my breathing, how a coma became my only reality.

How my mother waited.

I hadn't seen it coming. Maybe I should have. There had been signs: lingering pain from my immunotherapy treatments, a heaviness I couldn't shake, a deep exhaustion I had ignored. But I had chalked it up to motherhood, to travel, to life itself.

The past three months had been insane. The morning of my brain surgery began tenderly. Julian and I were snuggled up together at dawn, the sun not yet risen. I tried to hold on to that moment, just the two of us, before the day fully began. When the nanny arrived, I gathered my things and quietly stepped into the unfolding unknown.

Once at the hospital, I was quickly swept into a flurry of pre-op preparations: doctors, anesthesiologists, more explanations of what was to come. Then a resident appeared, holding an electric shaver. I looked at him wide-eyed. "What the hell is that?" I asked, more confused than alarmed at first. I knew they'd have to shave part of my head, but I assumed that would happen under anesthesia, not while I was awake and aware. But no, he explained that they needed to place electrodes in multiple areas to map the brain before surgery. I sat there as he shaved off random chunks of my hair, uneven and patchy, like some kind of deranged stylist. He didn't even clean up the clippings. I went in to feel this new rats' nest that was my hair and I remember looking at my mom and saying, "He left the hair in," my voice a strange mix of shock and disbelief. I felt like a living, breathing Cynthia doll. For those who know, you know.

Then came the antibiotics. They were administered through my IV, and almost immediately I could feel heat flooding my face. I told the team something wasn't right. "It's just Redman's Syndrome," someone reassured me, like it was no big deal. My face was beet red. My body was reacting. And yet, they assured me I'd be fine, "not ideal," but not life-threatening. So we pressed on.

Underneath it all, I was scared, really scared. I'd felt uneasy and anxious in the lead-up to surgery, but now that the moment had arrived, that anxiety bloomed into full-blown terror. "I'm about to have brain surgery," I kept thinking. My heart felt heavy, but I kept repeating to myself, "It's going to be okay." My mom stayed by my side, a grounding presence in the swirl of fear and fluorescent lights. Then, the surgery happened.

I woke up in the ICU, disoriented but functional. I could talk. I asked to take a walk as soon as I could. My brain had made it through, but my body had not forgotten what it was built to do. I was still producing milk. My breasts were painfully engorged, swollen, and sore. I needed a breast pump, but lacking that, I leaned on my best friend who helped me hand-express, something that was, at the same time, both deeply humbling and oddly sacred. My body was still showing up for my son, even as I lay in a hospital bed.

After one night in the ICU, I was moved to the Neuro floor. I asked my mom to bring me some pajamas, but in true mom fashion, she forgot. So my friends and I improvised. We crafted a toga out of hospital sheets. I'd request to take walks when the nurses made their rounds by my room, and one of them asked if I wanted to change. I looked at her blankly. "Like what do you mean? I look hot right now." I strutted up and down the halls like it was fashion week. When my oncologist passed by my room for a visit he even asked, "Is there a party happening here?" I replied without missing a beat, "Come join the party!"

Before discharge, I had to pass a few neurological exams. I was asked to rattle off as many animals as I could in under a minute. I started with the usual, cat, dog, then "Meerkat!" My friend laughed. Next was as many words that start with the letter "M." You best believe I started with meerkat. "Meerkat? Mongoose?" We cracked up. I felt proud of my brain. She had made it through.

After a few weeks of recovery, it was time to meet with my radiation oncologist. His office was dimly lit and... carpeted. Like... actual carpet. In a hospital. I couldn't get over it. Like the floor was trying to pretend this wasn't a sterile, high-stakes medical environment but instead your grandma's basement. I sat there thinking, is no one else weirded out by this? It felt like a design choice made by someone who had clearly never had to process the words "stereotactic radiation surgery."

My carpet fascination was soon interrupted by a far too chipper nurse who began rattling off questions before finally asking if I was still breastfeeding. When I said I'd had to stop, she replied, "Well, there's always the next one!" I stared at her, stunned. I'd just had brain surgery. I had lost something beautiful, intimate, and hard-earned, and she had the audacity to chirp about my 'next' child.

The oncologist explained that they'd be calculating my radiation dosage carefully to avoid necrosis and any sort of vital functions. The gravity of what that meant hit hard. This was my brain. Every treatment mattered.

To cope, I joked that I was heading off to space camp. My best friend even made me a "Rach Goes to Space Camp" playlist. I had to wear a tight, custom-fitted face mask to ensure precision during treatment. It was claustrophobic, uncomfortable, but I showed up. For five days in a row, I laid on a cold, hard table. On the first night, I woke up at 1 a.m., nauseous and vomiting. I had to get Zofran just to keep fluids down and still drag myself back for more treatment the next morning.

For the final session, I decided to wear a literal space suit. It was a running joke that started with my "wifey" a couple years prior, trying to bring lightness into something so heavy. I rang

74

the bell after my last radiation treatment, eyes full of unshed tears, heart full of unspeakable emotion. I couldn't even make eye contact with the nurses as I walked out. I had made it through the second phase. That's all that mattered.

Three to four weeks later, I'd begin immunotherapy. I'd been on this ride before. I knew to pre-medicate with Benadryl, and I thought I knew what to expect. The next day, I noticed my lymph nodes were swollen and tender. Concerned, I called the doctor on call. Her response? "Celebrate your body—it's responding! Take some Tylenol, you should be fine." It was oddly comforting, even if part of me still felt uneasy.

I was managing, but the weight of everything, scans, side effects, uncertainty, was adding up. I needed a change of scenery, a breath of fresh air, something that felt like life again. So, a couple of weeks later, bags packed and ready to go, we boarded a flight to Mexico.

When we arrived in Sayulita after a brief stop in Mexico City, I had felt an immediate pull to the place. The air was thick with salt and possibility, the streets buzzing with life. I had booked a surf lesson for later that afternoon, excited by the idea of riding waves, of proving to myself that my body was still capable, still mine.

But my body had other plans.

The seizure took me without warning, sending me face-first into the pool. One moment I was pushing Julian, the next I was gone.

When I woke up, my vision blurred, colors swimming in unnatural hues, like staring through a kaleidoscope that wouldn't stop turning. My limbs were heavy. My mind, a fog. I had the distinct sensation of being reborn, thinking I was a baby in a body too big for me.

Then my mother was there, her voice tethering me to something real. "You're okay," she said, though the tremor in her voice betrayed the words. "You're here."

But where was here? The last thing I remembered was booking a surf lesson. The last thing I remembered was the feel of Julian's tiny fingers gripping mine in the pool. What happened to me?

The truth was brutal. I had suffered a near-death seizure, intubated, kept under, hooked up to ventilators for three days. I had lost oxygen at one point. I had aspirated on my lunch and in the process of fishing out the food from my lungs, they punctured the lung and it collapsed, so they had to install a chest tube. Just another day in paradise.

No one had known what state I would wake up in, or if I would wake up at all. And when I did, I had to confront the terrifying reality that my body, once my own, was now unfamiliar terrain. I couldn't walk.

"Mom," I turned my head to face her.

"Where am I?"

"You're in the Punta Mita Hospital," my mom replied. "You had a seizure three days ago..."

I tried to shift in the bed. "Mom, I can't feel anything from the neck down."

I started to panic. Am I paralyzed?

It was the first thought that cut through the haze as I drifted back to consciousness, sharp, terrifying, impossible to ignore. My body felt heavy, unresponsive, like it belonged to someone else entirely. I tried to move a finger, a toe, anything, but nothing happened right away. A wave of dread surged through me.

I couldn't tell where my body ended and the bed began. I was trapped inside myself, suspended between dream and reality, unsure if the stillness was something I could break through, or if this was it. If I'd come back as a version of myself that couldn't move.

Tears pooled in my eyes, though even that felt distant, like my face had forgotten how to cry properly. My mind was racing. I had no idea how long I'd been like this, what had happened, or where I was. The last memory I had was sunlight on the pool and Julian's giggles.

The silence in the room was deafening. Machines hummed, a monitor beeped, someone shuffled nearby. But no one said the one thing I needed to hear: You're okay. You can move. You're going to be fine.

I was terrified to ask. Because what if I wasn't?

A doctor walked into the room right as I was mid-spiral.

"Oh good, you're awake."

"Doctor?" I could hardly utter words since even the littlest amount of effort would send me into a coughing fit.

"Will I be able to walk again?"

"Um... you should. We injected you with a high dose of steroids, so you should start to feel sensation in your arms. Not sure how long it'll take for you to regain sensation in your legs."

The thought was unsettling.

They told me I could order food. I opted for the chicken soup. Once it arrived and I began to eat, my hand trembled as it tried to reach my mouth. It almost felt like it'd be easier to try to fling the soup spoon than it was to move the spoon to reach my mouth. Eventually I think I slurped it. It was a deflating feeling. After I had eaten for the first time, I noticed a huge ache in my belly and knew I needed to use the restroom. I notified the nurses in the room, speaking to them in Spanish.

"Necesito ir al baño."

They replied that I had to go in my bed. What do you mean? Go in my bed?

They looked at me, calm and unbothered, and responded flatly: "Tienes que hacerlo en la cama."

I blinked, unsure I had heard them right. What do you mean, in the bed? I asked, hoping I had misunderstood, hoping this was a language barrier, not reality.

But no. I hadn't misunderstood. I was to go in the bed. Right there, under the blankets, on the crisp white sheets. Because I couldn't use my legs. Because I couldn't get up. Because, at that moment, I wasn't capable of doing something as basic and human as walking to a toilet. I tried to plead with them. They even showed me why it would not be possible. They tried to sit me up in the bed and my body flopped backwards once they let go.

It was one of the most humiliating moments of my life.

I wasn't just in a strange body. I was in a foreign country, in a strange hospital, and now I was being told to surrender whatever shred of dignity I had left. To do something I associated with babies, with helplessness, with total loss of autonomy. And I had no choice.

Tears welled in my eyes, not just from embarrassment but from the rawness of the reality I was facing. My body, which had carried a child and held so much strength, now couldn't even carry me to the bathroom.

There was no grace in that moment. Just surrender.

I shit the bed.

There's no poetic way to frame it. My body, stripped of its usual abilities and boundaries, did what it needed to do, and I laid there, powerless. I felt gross. Dirty. Not just physically, but existentially, like I had been reduced to something I didn't recognize, something barely human.

"¿Listo?" The nurses asked. "Listo," I could hardly reply.

The nurses cleaned me quickly, efficiently, like they'd done this a thousand times before. And I'm sure they had. But to me, it felt like a kind of death, a death of dignity, of self. I lay there, silent, tears slipping down the sides of my face, not from pain, but from something deeper. Shame. Helplessness. Grief for the version of myself I had lost.

Yes, I was alive. I made it. I'm still here. But in that moment, any version of gratitude felt like a distant planet, or another universe altogether. Somewhere far away, where people walked and stood and carried on about their day.

I wasn't ungrateful. I was just devastated. I had survived, but I didn't yet know what kind of life I was waking up into. And I didn't know if the person I had been before would ever fully return.

In a way I don't think this version of me ever returned. I was stepping into a new version of me. I was reborn, given another chance at life, and I held on to this sliver, this ember, small but burning, to rebuild and become the woman I was always meant to be. Not the version of me that existed before the seizure, before the coma, before the brain surgery or even the cancer diagnosis, but someone wiser, more tender, more fiercely alive.

It didn't come with fireworks or clarity. It came quietly, in flickers. In the moments I chose not to give up. In the breath I focused on when panic crept in. In the way I reached for my son, even when my arms trembled under their own weight. That ember, fragile, flickering, was all I had. But it was enough to begin again.

The first time they let me hold Julian again, I cried. Not a graceful, movie-scene tear, but a raw, silent sob that shook my already-fragile frame. Someone helped position my arms, carefully resting his little body against mine. He was heavier than I remembered, full of new life, soft and solid, so beautifully real.

For a moment, I stopped thinking about the machines, or the bruises on my arms, or whether I'd ever walk without help again. I stopped thinking about what I had lost. Because in that moment, I was just a mother holding her child. And somehow, that made everything feel possible.

I spent another two or three days in Punta Mita hospital before the airlift to the States was arranged. I had my own private jet, me, my mom, Julian, and a few handsome EMT guys. Not exactly the private jet experience I had once hoped for, but it was the one I got. I still had the chest tube with its lovely blood box attachment, monitors buzzing and beeping, scrunched into a stretcher like a human letter J.

Eventually, we touched down and I was checked into the ICU at Lutheran Hospital. They gave me a walker there, and each day, I got a little bit stronger. It felt like I was improving at astronomical speed. There was a special kind of strength kicking in, a mom strength. This wasn't just about getting better for me anymore.

For the first few days, I had a bed alarm and a bright yellow fall risk sign hanging outside my room. I couldn't believe it, thirty-one years old and a fall risk. Every time I swung my legs over the side of the bed, it was like an entire security team had to mobilize.

After a couple of days, they finally started trusting me to go to the bathroom alone, a major upgrade from the days of the bed alarm blaring if I so much as shifted in my sleep. I ditched the walker too, first shuffling down the hallway like a determined little grandma, then slowly finding my rhythm again.

At the same time, I was also hooked up to a continuous EEG, which meant I had dozens of electrodes glued to my scalp, each wire leading into a monitor that displayed my brain activity for someone, somewhere to quietly study behind the scenes. I may as well have been starring in a reboot of The Matrix, a tangled mess of cords and medical tape, staggering around the halls in my hospital gown. It was ridiculous. It was humbling. But it was also, in its own weird way, kind of triumphant.

Slowly but surely, the EEG monitor was shut down, the chest tube came out, and the IVs were removed. I started to feel less like a lab rat and more like a human again. The blood draws continued to happen daily. The phlebotomists would creep in and wake me at the ass crack of dawn, 4, sometimes 5am, the vampires. They were coming for me. I'd crack one eye open and reluctantly offer them an arm.

During physical and occupational therapy, they tailored exercises to help me get back to real life. One day they handed me a fifteen-pound sack and told me to pick it up off the ground, like picking up a baby from sitting to kneeling to standing. I got down, picked up the sack, then up on one knee and then... couldn't get up the rest of the way. I was stuck. The frustration hit hard. I fought it until the tears started slipping out. My physical therapist noticed and, without saying much, just took me downstairs for a coffee. No pep talks. No "stay positive" speeches. Just coffee. It was exactly what I needed.

Meanwhile, my first Mother's Day was creeping closer. I had recently gotten transferred to in-patient physical therapy and was supposed to stay there for additional time. I didn't care. I was done. I was over it. I was ready to go home.

My physical therapist, occupational therapist, and all the nurses were already on board. They were cheering for me, telling me I was ready. The last holdout was the rehab doctor, the head of PT. He was hesitant. It felt like all of us were trying to convince him. I think even the nurses were side-eyeing him to get with the program. Eventually, he agreed. It felt like winning a small but mighty battle.

Sunday morning, I was discharged. They wheeled me to the hospital entrance, because that was protocol, but the second I saw the car, I stood up from the wheelchair and walked, practically ran toward it. I grabbed my legs underneath my thighs to lift them into the car. My mom looked at me, wide-eyed and worried, but I just smiled and said, "Don't worry. They're strong."

It wasn't graceful, it wasn't perfect, but I didn't care. I was coming home to my baby for our first Mother's Day together, and that was everything.

8

∞

WHILE I WAS IN THE HOSPITAL, I missed Julian more than anything. The ache of that separation was constant. I worried about the impact of what he had witnessed during my seizure, how that might live in his little body and memory, but I was also deeply grateful that he had been safe in that moment, that my mom had been there to pull me from the water and save my life. In the first few days of my hospital stay once I was stateside, COVID restrictions were still in place, and I couldn't see him, which made everything harder. But after a couple of days, they lifted the restrictions, and my mom was finally able to bring him to see me. When he saw me, he lit up. It felt like medicine for both of us. Those brief visits gave me life, tiny, normal moments in a world that had turned into a full-blown shitshow. Those moments, or glimmers, were everything.

Glimmers, the opposite of triggers. In contrast to triggers, which activate the nervous system's threat response, glimmers signal safety and regulation. Coined by Deb Dana in the context of polyvagal theory, glimmers are small, often subtle experiences that evoke a sense of calm, connection, or joy. They help the brain and body remember what it feels like to be safe, to be okay. They don't erase the hard stuff, but they anchor us. They remind us what we're fighting for and what's still possible, even when everything feels like it's falling apart. For me, holding Julian was one of the most powerful glimmers. I'd pull him into my arms, his little fingers curled around mine, and look into his eyes. In those quiet moments of connection, I remembered what really mattered. What was worth getting up for. He was my glimmer in the storm.

By the time I made it home, I was walking and even climbing stairs, slowly but surely rebuilding strength. But because my punctured lung was still healing, everything took more effort. I started outpatient physical therapy, followed by a pulmonary rehab program, and had to use an inhaler twice a day. It was like starting from scratch, physically. Pulmonary was where I met Nancy and Sally, the two sweet older women who made me feel less alone. Their warmth, humor, and gentle presence reminded me that even in the most unexpected places, you can find connection. That in this weird, insurance-approved classroom, we were there for each other. And instead of sharing markers and whatever was in our lunchboxes, we bonded over pulse oximeters.

I remember the sideways glances from some of the others. What's this thirty-something doing here? "Did she somehow wander into the wrong room?" But Nancy and Sally put me at ease. At the beginning, walking at just 3 mph on the treadmill would spike my pulse, but by the end, I had started jogging and Sally would come over and call me a show-off, and we'd both laugh. That laughter, that small sense of sass she'd throw my way was its own kind of healing. I know she was proud of me; I was proud of myself too.

It was a couple of months before I could return to immunotherapy infusions after my seizure at the end of April, or as I also refer to it, "the accident." My next infusion didn't happen until late June, and it was important that I keep going. Even with everything that had happened, I couldn't just stop, but my body did need time to regain strength. I had a gnarly cough from the pneumonitis, and then, just to keep things interesting, I developed colitis at the end of May. There was a full-on fire raging inside my body. And they couldn't just throw a saline pouch full of intense drugs on it and hope for the best. They had to put the fire out first before adding anything else to the mix.

My daily cocktail became a steady mix of anti-seizure meds, prednisone, and an inhaler. Immunotherapy infusions continued once a month for the next year. They were something I had to go through, but they weren't the center of my universe anymore. I'd learned to manage the side effects as they came, tucking them into the rhythm of daily life.

What became central was regaining my strength, not just for me, but for Julian. Physical therapy was grueling, humbling, and deeply transformative. I brought his car seat to one of my appointments, and my therapist loaded it with a 15-pound sack. My job was to carry it down the hall and back. And I did. A little shaky, a little out of breath, but I did it. Every session was a reminder that not only was I recovering, I was also rebuilding and rewiring. And at the root of it all was my motivation to be the best mother I could be, and to feel safe and strong in my own skin again.

Then one day, a sponsored ad popped up on my Instagram feed: ballroom dance. I clicked it, curious, and saw the studio was less than ten minutes from my house. I wasn't ready yet, but I bookmarked it. Followed the account. Started liking their posts. A silent promise to myself: When I'm ready, I'll come back to this.

I didn't know it at the time, but dance would help me find my way home. Home to my body, to joy, to something beyond the identity of patient or even mother. When the time came, dancing became about more than movement. It was a full-bodied yes to life. A way to trust myself again. A way to feel free.

When I finally walked into that dance studio, I wasn't just signing up to take a class. I was reclaiming something that felt lost, my connection to joy, to presence, to my body. I wasn't there to impress anyone. I was there to move, to feel, and to trust that I still lived somewhere underneath the scans and setbacks.

The studio was simple, but it held a quiet kind of magic: one open room with wooden floors, a mirrored wall that reflected every movement, and a moveable ballet barre tucked in the back corner. It smelled faintly of wood and effort, the kind of place shaped by repetition and heart. And always, there was a little Yorkie (Starboy), tail wagging, bouncing with excitement, ready to greet me at the door like I belonged there.

The mirrors didn't scare me the way I thought they might. Instead of seeing a broken version of who I used to be, I saw a woman who had survived, who was choosing to show up for herself, for her son, and for life. Step by step, rhythm by rhythm, I felt pieces of myself start to fuse back together. This time not in a hospital, but on a dance floor.

When I first showed up, Krystian, my dance instructor, took one look at me wobbling across the floor and called me "Bambi on ice." I laughed, because he wasn't wrong. I figured I'd try one lesson, and see how it felt. The next thing I knew, I was handing my credit card over for four more lessons... then sixteen. Then even more.

For my second lesson, I'd shown up in rinky-dink, $30 heels from Amazon. They worked, barely, until they didn't. Soon I was ordering $300 professional dance shoes like this was something I did. At my third lesson, Krystian asked me what my dance goals were. I shrugged. To dance? To have fun? Then he asked, "Do you want to compete?" I hadn't thought about it before. But maybe.

The dollar amount didn't matter anymore. Dance had become essential to my well-being. I felt alive in that studio. It was lighthearted, playful, a space where I could leave my worries at the door and just be. In that mirrored room, I reconnected with my body in a way I hadn't felt in a long time. I became more autonomous, more at home in myself.

Ballroom dance became my therapy in motion, a space where I could be fully in my body without needing to explain it.

It helped me rewrite the narrative from "Look what I've lost" to "Look at what I've found." It wasn't always easy though. I had to work hard to not get frustrated when my body couldn't move the way I wanted it to or when I'd lose my balance. But the discipline it required also reminded me of something I had once deeply valued: breathwork and meditation.

Before and during pregnancy, I had been meditating daily, sometimes for an hour at a time. From the beginning of COVID I was a part of a virtual meditation group that would meet twice a week. But then, life sped up. I became a mom, I got busy, and meditation quietly fell to the bottom of the list. Now, as I rebuilt physical strength, I knew these practices were life-changing when I committed to them.

I stopped focusing on perfection or big goals. This wasn't about becoming some serene guru or activating and aligning my chakras. It was about reclaiming space for myself. Instead of disappearing into a scroll hole, I carved out those moments to be still, connect with the body, quiet the mind, and remember what it felt like to be fully present in my own skin.

So, right now, while you're reading or listening to my book, I invite you to pause for a moment of stillness yourself. Take a deep breath in through your nose, fill your lungs with air. Exhale fully through the mouth. Take another deep breath, allow your belly to expand, hold it for a moment, take another sip of air. Sigh it out through your mouth. One more deep breath in through your nose. Fully, fully exhale out through your mouth and allow your belly to hug towards your spine. Now breathe in and out through the nose a few times, full belly breaths in and out through the nose. And voilà! That's a quick meditation you can come back to over and over again. I've included a resources section in the back of the book with additional meditations as well.

I didn't always believe in meditation. For a long time, I thought it was just sitting in silence pretending not to think, and I wasn't sure how that was supposed to do anything. I was curious about it, sure, but skeptical. It wasn't until I did my yoga teacher training that I actually committed to it in a real way: daily practice, extended sessions, full immersion. And that's when it finally clicked. I started to notice subtle shifts: how I responded instead of reacted, how I could sit with discomfort without needing to fix it, how my breath could tether me when the rest of me felt like it was floating away. It didn't change my life overnight, but it changed my relationship to life. And that was enough to keep going.

Even after that, my practice had seasons, periods of discipline followed by stretches where it all fell away. After Julian was born, I found my way back again. I rejoined the virtual meditation group and began carving out time when I could, even during breastfeeding sessions; anything can be a meditation. But eventually, as life got heavier, it slipped away once more. Surgery, treatment schedules, recovery. It all edged meditation out, as survival became the focus. And yet, every time I came back to it, even for five or ten minutes, I remembered why it mattered.

Meditation helped me re-center, not in some lofty, spiritual bypass kind of way, but in a real, grounded way. Much like dance reconnected me to my body's strength, meditation reconnected me to my inner steadiness. It helped me meet fear with presence, and it reminded me of who I was underneath the noise.

That said, I've come to realize that meditation isn't a cure-all. There's a version of spirituality out there that can be dangerous, one that insists if you just meditate consistently or think positively enough, you can bypass real pain or real illness. I've even heard people say you shouldn't take medicine, or shouldn't trust doctors, that if you just align your energy, everything will be fine.

While maybe some people have been able to "meditate it away," that narrative can be slightly toxic. It creates this illusion that if you're sick, it's because you're not aligned enough or not trying hard enough. And if you do choose treatment, it can stir up guilt or shame, like you've failed some kind of spiritual test. I say this because I felt it.

I'm here to say: you didn't do anything wrong. If you chose medicine, you didn't fail. If you tried the natural route and it didn't work, you didn't fail. If you meditated and journaled and visualized healing and still got sick, you didn't do anything wrong. Illness isn't a punishment, and healing isn't a reward for being good enough or spiritual enough. It's not your fault. We're all just doing our best to survive and to live well, in the bodies we've been given, with the cards we've been dealt.

I believe in letting the tools of meditation and medicine work together: body, mind, spirit, medicine, movement. It's not either/or. It's both/and. For me, healing is about integration, not exclusion.

After everything I'd been through, I started to feel something deeper settle in me, an understanding that God, or the divine, or the universe, whatever name you give it, can be found in everything. Not just in quiet prayers or meditation cushions, but in the mess and motion of life. In medicine. In surgeons. In the hands that held mine when I was afraid. In the science and system that kept me breathing. In the nurse's kindness, the dance studio, the ocean, the coconut water, the tiny fingers of my child wrapped around mine.

There's this story I've always loved, the one about the man standing on a cliff during a massive flood. He prays to God to save him. A boat comes, he waves it away. Then a helicopter, he refuses again. "God will save me," he says. But he drowns. And when he meets God in the afterlife, he asks, "Why didn't you save me?" And God says, "I sent you a boat, I sent you a helicopter. What more did you want?"

That's how I've come to understand it. God, life, it shows up in every form. Sometimes in unexpected ways. We don't have to choose between science and spirit. We can use it all. Trust it all. Pull in every tool we've got. And in doing so, we honor that sacred force moving through everything, and within us, as well.

At this point in my life, I was focused on living well, really living. I spent time with friends and took a couple of trips with my mom and Julian. There was a newfound joy and deep gratitude woven into everything I did. Watching Julian explore and grow, and navigate the world with curiosity, felt especially meaningful. In many ways, I saw myself in him, both of us learning to find our footing, one breath at a time, on this strange green and blue rock spinning through space.

Later that year in November, my mom, Julian and I took a trip to Italy. We explored the ancient cobblestone streets and ate all the things. It felt like a celebration, a memory I'll always hold close. Not long after, when Julian was fifteen months old, we returned to Tulum for the first time following my seizure. It was surreal. The same turquoise waves rolling in and retreating, as though the earth was inhaling and exhaling with each wave, and the same breeze rustling through the palms. Life had carried on, unchanged by the chaos that had turned my world upside down. That contrast, how steady the world could be, even when my body and soul was integrating and recalibrating, felt weird, but it was also everything I needed. I watched Julian drink coconut water straight from a coconut, his face sticky and smiling. I watched him sit on the beach and dig into chips and guac like it was the best thing he'd ever tasted. These simple moments, sun, sand, and a guac-stained face, reminded me that joy still existed. Even though my life was still peppered with monthly infusions and follow-up MRIs, I was focused on living fully. I wasn't waiting for peace to arrive. I was finding it in the in-between.

Life was wild, to say the least. The treatments, the PT, the dance lessons, all while raising a toddler. It was a lot. It was busy. But it was all so, so beautiful.

I kept a countdown until my final treatment: five left, now four, three, two... last one. I was inching toward the finish line. I even dusted off the old space suit and wore it to my final infusion in March 2024. Phase 3: complete. I was done. At last, the storm had passed. I let myself exhale.

9

∞

"WE'RE GONNA NEED TO DO ANOTHER BRAIN SURGERY."
    I stared at my neurosurgeon, stunned. You're joking. A second brain surgery? I had just recovered from the first one. My hair had just grown in. Who has one brain surgery in their life, let alone two? I was still trying to process it when he left the room and his assistant walked in to get me on the books. They scheduled it for the following week, Memorial Day weekend. I was devastated.
    My mom and I left the hospital in a daze, and as soon as we got to the car, I called my best friend. The moment she picked up, I broke down sobbing. I could barely get the words out. I thought I was done with all of this, the surgeries, the trauma, the fear. I thought peace was finally within reach.

At that point, I had been getting MRIs every three months. The March scan following my final immunotherapy infusion showed swelling around one of the brain lesions, the same one that had hemorrhaged the year before and triggered the seizure. My oncologist wasn't worried though. He said it was likely immunotherapy-related and that it should calm down now that treatment was done. "Let's just repeat it in a month."

In April, we did. Same swelling. Again: "It's only been a month. Let's give it more time."

Now off immunotherapy, I had started tapering off the prednisone, had ditched the inhaler, and was even training for my first ballroom dance competition. I was feeling good, hopeful, and then came May 10th.

I was driving home from the city after a girlfriend's birthday, cruising down the freeway, when suddenly, something didn't feel right. My right leg, the one on the gas pedal, had gone completely numb, like a dead weight. A lead foot.

I managed to pull over to the shoulder and brake with my left foot. I put the car in park and called my mom. "You need to call 9-1-1," she said.

I'd never called 9-1-1 on myself before. I held my right leg in my hands, hoping it would come back to life while I tried to explain my location. "I'm on 90/94," I said. "Which one?" the dispatcher asked. "Uh... I don't know. Can't you GPS this or something?" My brain was spinning. "Okay, 90, no wait... 94. I'm by the Dempster exit." "Going east or westbound?"

Then the seizing started. My leg began to spasm and jerk, and the pain was excruciating.

"Ow, fuck, fuck, fuck." "East or westbound?" the dispatcher asked again. "West. I'm on the shoulder," I gasped, trying to take deep breaths through the pain. The dispatcher kept me on the line. "We're sending an ambulance. Just stay with me."

A few minutes later, I saw the flashing lights in my rearview mirror. The ambulance pulled up in front of me, and by that time, the seizing had stopped. I was able to get out and walk to them. They took my vitals, blood sugar normal, BP 135/90. I said that was high for me. "Well, you've just had a pretty stressful event," they replied. "That's normal by our standards."

They offered to take me to the hospital, but left the decision up to me, explaining, "You seem fine to us. How do you feel?" I was a little shaken up, but felt fine at that point. A sheriff then stepped into the ambulance, gave me a once-over, and said, "She seems fine to me." She asked how far from home I was, and since I was only 20 minutes away, that was that. They let me go.

Honestly, I thought maybe someone would follow me home, just in case, but nope. The ambulance pulled away. I got back in my car and drove myself home. Safely.

It was around 10 p.m. when I finally arrived home, rattled, but in one piece. Sleep didn't come easily that night. I found myself thinking about the gut feeling I'd had earlier that afternoon, the weird feeling I'd had that I should bail on the birthday party and stay home instead. I'm not sure why I ignored it, and I wonder what might have happened had I gone that route instead. I'm also incredibly grateful that my angels and guides kept me safe that night.

Intuition is a funny thing. I've come to see it almost like a muscle that we need to practice, one that once stronger, helps us hear our inner messages. And then, when we lean into cultivating it, and strengthening it, it helps us distinguish the difference between what is actually a fear that will only hold us back, versus an inner knowing that comes to the surface to guide our way.

Our intuition rarely screams at us. Instead, it tends to show up as a soft whisper. It nudges us. Paying attention to it is much like tending a garden, in that it requires patience and trust in what can't always be seen right away.

There are some ways we can flex and strengthen our intuitive muscles though. Here are some examples:

1. Create Quiet Space. Intuition speaks softly. It's hard to hear it over the noise of constant scrolling, endless to-dos, or the opinions of others. Even just five minutes a day of stillness, through meditation, breathwork, a walk in nature, or just sitting in silence, can open up space to hear the whispers.

2. Pay Attention To The Body. Intuition often shows up physically before it becomes a conscious thought. A flutter in the chest, a pit in your stomach, tightness in your throat. These sensations often carry meaning. The more we pay attention to how our body reacts to certain people, places, and decisions, the more attuned we become to our inner compass.

3. Practice Asking And Listening. Ask yourself small questions and see what naturally arises. "Do I want to go to this event?" or "What would bring me peace today?" Practice noticing your first response, the one that comes up before your rational brain kicks in to argue with it.

4. Reflect Through Journaling. Writing down your thoughts can help you spot patterns. You might notice you "knew" something before it happened, or that a choice which didn't make logical sense ended up being right for you. The more you acknowledge those moments, the more you build trust in your own inner knowing.

5. Limit Outside Noise. It's tempting to poll everyone you know before making a big decision. But too many outside voices can drown out your own. When you catch yourself outsourcing clarity, pause. Ask yourself what you think or feel before turning to others.

6. Revisit Times You Did Listen. Think back to moments when following your gut led to something good, even if it didn't make sense at the time. These stories are evidence. Reminders that you can trust yourself.

7. Stay Grounded. Intuition isn't the same as anxiety, projection, or spiraling worst-case scenarios. That's why grounding practices, like movement, deep breathing, or connecting with nature, help keep the channel clear so you can discern true intuition from fear or overthinking.

Intuition isn't a one-and-done kind of thing. It's not a switch you flip once and then always get it "right." There will be times when you go against it, miss it completely, or feel unsure if what you're sensing is fear, gut instinct, or just noise. And that's okay. Learning to trust your intuition is just that, a practice. It takes time, patience, and compassion for yourself. Sometimes the lesson is in following it. Other times, the growth comes from ignoring it and learning what that felt like in hindsight. Either way, you build trust not by always getting it right, but by showing up again and again, listening more closely each time.

Little did I know how deeply I'd have to tap into, and trust, my inner compass in the weeks to come. After what happened on my return from the birthday party that night, I called my care team. I needed some answers. What the fuck had just happened, and why?

My neurologist explained that the swelling in my brain was likely the culprit, specifically in the region that controls sensorimotor function in my right leg. We moved my May MRI up to the earliest available date. In the meantime, she told me to increase both my anti-seizure meds and my prednisone dosage. I was less than thrilled because I was supposed to be tapering off the prednisone, not increasing the dosage again, but I obliged.

I went in for my MRI on May 23rd, and then saw my neurosurgeon a few days later. He pulled up the images and sat in silence, scrolling, adjusting the contrast, studying every pixel. Then he swiveled around in his chair and said, matter-of-factly, "Yep, we'll need to get rid of it."

"Get rid of what?" I thought to myself... my brain? I was pretty sure I'd need that.

And then, as I grappled with the idea of a second brain surgery, beneath the panic and the heartbreak, I heard a small voice inside whisper to me: maybe there's another way.

So I started researching, and went in search of a second opinion. I booked an appointment at the Mayo Clinic, but the earliest they could see me was the end of June, so I turned elsewhere. Rush University had an opening at the beginning of July, and then I found the University of Chicago. They could get me in the first week of June. That was my quickest shot, so I set up back-to-back appointments with their oncologist and neurosurgeon.

The oncologist went over my scans and, like my previous team, said I'd likely need surgery. My mom and I left that appointment and took a walk along the lake at Promontory Point, trying to take in the air, the view, and the weight of it all. I had started to accept it. Two out of three doctors were telling me the same thing, another brain surgery was in the cards. I just about canceled the neurosurgeon appointment. What was the point? But something told me to keep it.

I met with the neurosurgery resident the next day, and we pulled up my scans, the ones I'd seen so many times I could practically recite them from memory. He studied them for a while, then looked at me and said, "Well, yes, you could have another craniotomy. Or you're also a good candidate for a much less invasive option. We'd take a biopsy through a small hole, about a quarter the size of a McDonald's straw, and then use a laser to ablate the lesion." I suddenly felt hopeful. It seemed that voice inside me, the one that had whispered there might be another way, had been right after all.

The neurosurgeon told me they'd need to present my case to the tumor board for approval first, but if they agreed, I'd be good to go. A few days later, I got the call: the board had given the green light, and my surgery was scheduled for the following week. Yes, it was still brain surgery, but at least I wasn't going to have my skull sliced open and stapled shut this time. I could handle this. I got this.

I even wore a T-shirt on the day of surgery that said, "You got this." I brought my cat unicorn Squishmallow pillow for comfort and went through the usual routine: hospital gown, allergy rundown, IVs placed, and did my best to stay grounded. Before I knew it (obviously), I was waking up in post-op recovery.

To my surprise, I felt okay. There was barely any pain. Naturally, my first question was: how much hair did they shave off? I couldn't see the spot right away since it was bandaged, but when they removed the gauze the next morning, I saw it: a teeny-tiny stitch surrounded by a comically large bald circle. Really? Did they really have to shave that much hair? It was a girl resident I had spoken to the day before about the hair shaving. Girl to girl, I thought she'd have my back.

I stayed one night in the hospital and was discharged the next day. But before I left, something happened that really stuck with me. The night nurse tried to administer my antibiotic through a bad IV site. The pain was immediate and excruciating. I yelped for him to stop, but he didn't. It wasn't until my mom stepped in, "Can't you hear her? She's telling you to stop," that he finally listened.

I hadn't thought about it before, but afterward, I read about how many patients equate medical trauma to a kind of violation. That's exactly what it felt like. I ended up needing a pain med, not for the brain surgery, but for the IV, an irony that wasn't lost on me. But for all that, I was grateful, grateful the surgery itself went as smoothly as it did.

Soon I was back home, relieved to be with my little man, rocking a bald spot I tried to comb over in a way that was, admittedly, a little Trump-esque. The important thing was, I was home, and I was healing.

During this time, I was also hosting monthly sound meditations, something that had always brought me peace, but now felt like a deeper offering. If you've never been to one, this is what it's like: I play a mix of crystal sound bowls, a gong, and other instruments I've gathered from different corners of the world. Each session is designed to bathe the body in healing vibrational frequencies, helping people relax, de-stress, and return to themselves. Holding that space for others is a kind of medicine for me, too, a reminder that healing can ripple outward, even when you're still putting your own pieces back together.

Even in the aftermath of everything I'd been through, I could still create beauty, still hold space, and still continue to heal. Because the thing about healing is, it's not about taking you back to the person you once were. It's about rising from the ashes, more powerful than you were before.

10

AS I WAS HOLDING SPACE for others, I realized it might be time to try holding space for myself in a new way, by letting someone else in.

Where else was a single mom supposed to turn? The dating apps. Naturally. I downloaded Bumble and started swiping, already rolling my eyes at how superficial it felt. I'd been on and off the apps for a while: download, delete, repeat. Like a digital version of "eat, sleep, rinse, repeat." I wasn't convinced I'd meet anyone meaningful this way, but this time felt different. I felt different.

It wasn't just that I'd had my heart broken enough times to qualify for some kind of loyalty punch card. I'd faced a near-death seizure, had much of my hair shaved off in exchange for a titanium plate, rebuilt my body, and learned to trust it again. I'd stood on competition floors and hospital floors. I'd grown a tiny human and survived brain surgery. Twice.

I was more intentional. I didn't have the time, or the energy, for small talk, breadcrumbing, or men who weren't clear about what they wanted, because I was no longer dating just for myself. I was dating as a mother, which is a whole different ball game. I knew I wanted to be in a relationship. Not just for me, but for Julian too.

A quiet thought sat in the back of my mind as I swiped. My little boy might one day look to this relationship as an example of what love, respect, and emotional maturity look like. Pre-baby, all I considered was: Do I like him? But now? The question was: Do I like him enough to consider whether he'd be a good influence on my toddler? Because at the end of the day, I had another tiny human in my life, one who might someday watch how this man treats me and internalize it as the blueprint.

So yes, I was vetting for more than just chemistry this time. I was scanning for safety, softness, consistency, and the ability to use emotional language that wasn't just "yeah, vibes."

That's a lot of pressure to put on a man whose profile picture shows him holding a dead fish.

As I swiped past gym selfies, group pics where I had no idea who was who, and baby photos captioned "not my kid," one thought lingered in the back of my mind: how is this the modern path to love? I was looking for the real thing, with real depth, real presence, and ideally, no fish photos in their profile. I still wanted the spark, but I also wanted someone who texted back in full sentences and didn't flinch at the word "commitment."

For a long time, I'd kept my heart guarded. Past experiences had taught me that letting someone in often meant dimming my own light for the sake of the other person. But something in me was shifting. I was no longer willing to live from fear. Maybe healing hadn't made me fearless, but it had made me ready. I'd walked through the fire and survived. I'd become a new version of myself. I wasn't dating for fun. I was dating with purpose, clarity, and the kind of inner strength you only earn when you go through hell and come out the other side... still dancing. I was looking for something real.

Okay, so I'm not perfect. One of the first guys I matched with, and actually started dating, was hot. Like, really hot. The kind of hot where I maybe... temporarily forgot my list of non-negotiables and rationalized a couple red flags. Baby steps, okay? We dated for a few months, but eventually parted ways. Our values didn't align, and while it wasn't dramatic, it also wasn't it. Civil, cordial, no bad blood. Just... not the one.

Then came guy number two. Seemed like a nice guy. Normal. Decent. We had three dates, good conversation, easy vibe, and then he completely ghosted me. Like, vanished. No explanation, no closure, nothing. It was so fucking weird. And because I couldn't help myself, I sent a text even though I knew I'd been ghosted:

"Ghosting? 1 ⭐ If I could leave zero stars, I would. If you weren't feeling the connection, I wish you'd just said so." As expected: no response.

Let's talk about ghosting for a second.

Because here's the thing, being ghosted sucks. It's more than just someone vanishing mid-conversation. It's the sudden absence that hits right after you let your guard down just enough to imagine that maybe this one's different. That maybe this could go somewhere. You give a little spark of hope, nothing crazy, just a flicker, and then... poof. Gone. No explanation, no closure. Just your own brain playing detective, trying to piece together the crime scene of a conversation that was alive one day and radio silent the next.

It's not just rejection. It's erasure. Like someone looked at your humanity and said, "Eh. Pass."

No wonder people delete the apps. And then re-download them a week later. It's the modern romance loop: swipe, match, talk, hope, ghost, delete, repeat. I had been on and off the apps so many times, only to return like some emotionally resilient goldfish with amnesia. Because deep down, I still wanted to believe in connection. And let's be honest, single parenting doesn't exactly flood your social calendar with hot prospects.

To be honest, when I matched with guy number three, I had gotten to the point where I was losing hope. Maybe it just wasn't meant to happen right now. I almost bailed, but something within me told me to go for it.

To paint a picture, his profile didn't exactly scream "this is your soulmate." His main photo was a slightly faraway shot of him lounging in a hammock. Okay, maybe he's outdoorsy? I'm into it. His bio read: "Actually 3'7" in heels," which I thought was cute and funny. There were a couple of decent selfies... and then, there it was: the pig costume. Full body. No context. Just... him. Dressed as a pig. But something about his energy, his humor, the lightness in the way our messages flowed... it pulled me in.

Our chats felt playful, easy. Thoughtful. When he found out I danced, he planned a dance lesson for our first date. The day before he didn't ask, "Hey, are we still on?" That would have given me an easy out, but instead he sent me the address and time to meet him.

If you know anything about ballroom dancing, it's intimate. You're close, really close. So yeah... we got comfortable pretty quickly. He only stepped on my feet a couple of times, but I didn't mind. There was something endearing about it, like he was trying but not performing. He was fully present.

And just like that, something opened.

Neither of us wanted the night to end, so we walked over to the brewery next door and kept talking. But it wasn't just the usual "what do you do?" surface-level stuff. It was deeper. Heartfelt. The kind of conversation that reminds you you're still capable of connecting in that way. Of being seen.

When it came time to close out our tab, the bartender struck up a conversation and somehow we landed on the topic of celebrity doppelgängers. I got Sarah Palin, which, okay, ouch. But then he got... Jeffrey Dahmer.

What better way to impress your date than to be casually likened to a serial killer?

We laughed. A bunch. And not just about the doppelgänger thing. There was a lightness between us that felt rare. Like for the first time in a long time, I didn't have to carry it all. I could just... be.

Right before our second date, I got a message from him saying he'd be running late. Not a big deal. I replied, "No problem." Then another message popped up:

"I also left without putting shoes on, so I had to turn around. Phone says I'll be there at 11:22."

I stared at the screen, unsure what to make of it. Left the house without shoes? Like... did he not notice his bare feet hit the pavement? Or the gas and brake pedals on his drive? I had questions.

But when we met up, he explained he'd left wearing his house Crocs instead of his gym shoes. Okay. That felt better. Slightly more functional. Still hilarious.

And that's the thing, there was something about these small moments that made me feel even more at ease. He wasn't trying to impress me with perfection. He was just showing up as he was: thoughtful, imperfect, himself. It matched the way our relationship was beginning to unfold, honest, direct, and full of intention. He made me feel safe. Not just with his words, but in the way he saw me, and in the way he didn't try to play it cool or keep things vague.

About a month in, he asked me to be his girlfriend. No assumptions, no blurred lines. Just a question, clearly spoken, waiting for an answer. Loving him was effortless. Not because everything's always easy, but because the foundation felt real. Because I could exhale around him.

Communication used to feel scary. Like walking on eggshells, carefully choosing my words, anticipating a defensive response, and somehow still ending up the one apologizing. Cue the gaslighting. Sharing how I felt often led to disconnection, not closeness.

But here, with him, it felt different. It felt safe.

I could bring something up, something real, something vulnerable, and instead of walls going up, we would move closer. There was space for honesty, for repair if needed, for understanding without power plays. The conversations didn't drain me. They nourished me.

When we spent time together it felt familiar in the best way. Like something I had always deserved but didn't quite believe I could have.

Introducing him to Julian felt natural, like the next right step, not some huge milestone I had to overthink. He was the first guy I'd ever brought around my son, but somehow it didn't feel loaded or nerve-wracking. It felt grounded. Like I trusted not just him, but also myself and the space we were building.

And watching their relationship begin to unfold was its own kind of beautiful. Julian has always been intuitive, tuned in in ways that feel beyond his years, and he took to this new person quickly, offering up his toys, his tiny way of saying, you can be part of my world. There was no forcing it.

And in witnessing Julian's seemingly easy acceptance, I realized I trusted his judgment too. That's the thing with kids. They don't fake comfort. They don't perform affection. They just feel what they feel, and I could see that Julian felt safe. He laughed. He shared. He reached for his hand. And I paid attention.

In many ways, he mirrored back what I was beginning to feel myself: that this was someone who could be let in. That we were safe here. Trusting him helped me trust myself. And maybe that's what this chapter of my life is really about, learning to listen to the quiet instincts I'd once silenced, and realizing that love, when it's real, doesn't demand that you shrink. It invites you to expand.

11

MY ALARM RANG at the ungodly hour of 5:20 a.m. "Do I have time to snooze? Maybe 10 more minutes." When the alarm rang again at 5:30 a.m., I rubbed my groggy eyes, stumbled out of my hotel room, into the elevator, and made my way downstairs.

During hair and makeup, my nerves buzzed, but more with excitement than fear. I slipped into a sleek, yet flowy black dress that hugged me in all the right places, simple but elegant, with just enough shimmer to catch the light when I moved. For the first time in a long time, I didn't just look like a dancer. I felt like one.

I made my way out of the dressing room and headed upstairs to the grand ballroom. There was music and the sound of heels on polished floors. I warmed up, stretched, and steadied my breath. This wasn't just about winning or performing. It was about showing up for myself, claiming space, owning my story, and moving with intention in a body that had carried me through so much.

And there, in the audience, was my new boyfriend. Cheering me on. Beaming. Holding space in the most unobtrusive, supportive way. Just being there. I caught his eye before I stepped out onto the floor, and something in his smile said, I see you.

I poured everything I had into my dancing, every ounce of my energy and soul into each step like never before. The adrenaline still buzzed through me as we waited for the awards ceremony to begin.

By noon, all the dances had wrapped up, and we gathered around the sweaty dance floor, anticipation hanging heavy in the air. Then the judges announced my name.

I had won second place. It was a moment I'll never forget.

I nearly cried. Who am I kidding, I did cry. Not because of the medal or the ranking, but because I was remembering the days I could barely walk without pain. The days I could hardly breathe without huffing and puffing. The days I didn't recognize myself in the mirror. The days I wasn't sure I'd ever feel joy in my body again.

This wasn't just a dance competition. It was a reclamation. Of beauty. Of movement. Of self. Afterwards, my boyfriend and I celebrated the only way that made sense, with dumplings. The most delicious dumplings. Ever. As one should.

We sat across from each other at a tiny table, steam rising between us, dipping sauces everywhere. He looked at me with that steady, curious gaze and asked, "So... how are you feeling? Did you have fun?"

I paused. "I think so," I replied, half-laughing, half-questioning.

Because the truth was, I was so proud of myself. But it had also been... brutal. The 5:30 a.m. wake-up, the adrenaline surges, the anxiety shits between rounds (glamorous, I know). On top of that, there was the stress of remembering steps and making it all look effortless while my heart tried to punch its way out of my chest.

I loved dancing. I loved what it gave me, the freedom, the connection, the joy. But competing? I wasn't so sure.

Still, there was something about that day that stayed with me. The effort. The risk. The aliveness of it all. Even in the exhaustion, I felt like I'd cracked open a new part of myself. And that deserved to be honored, with dumplings and laughter, and shared with someone who didn't need me to be perfect. Just real.

Returning to everyday life was... interesting, to say the least. I was excited about my upcoming three-month trip to Tulum, but before I could fully lean into that dream, there was still a storm cloud looming on the edge of everything. As much as I didn't want to have to deal with this one, it demanded resolution: the lesion my care team had been keeping a close eye on.

It was tucked near the original surgical cavity in my brain, close to my visual cortex. Back in June 2024, it had measured 3mm, but by September, it had grown to 6mm. They scheduled me for surgery on Labor Day weekend, about a month before Julian's second birthday. No one on the team was entirely convinced it was a tumor. It was to be a prophylactic surgery, "just in case," because I wasn't showing any symptoms.

I started seeing a healer, because yes, I still believe and continue to believe in alternative treatments as well as western medicine. And, after consulting with my neurologist and neuroradiologist, I made the call to cancel. We would reassess after my next scan.

The following month the scan showed a slight decrease, measuring at about 5mm, enough of a decrease to give us confidence in holding off. But then, in early November, the lesion appeared to have grown, measuring 6mm once again, so they rescheduled the surgery for the day before Thanksgiving.

I began to emotionally prepare, and had started to accept another surgery was in the cards, but no matter how ready I tried to feel, the questions in my mind remained. I kept asking myself and my care team: Was it really worth putting myself through another surgery for something that seemed to be stable and asymptomatic? Was the risk of intervention greater than the risk of waiting?

Ultimately, I decided to cancel. Again. And this time, everyone was on board. I got the green light to leave for Mexico for three months. A gift I didn't take lightly. And spoiler alert, there were no near-death seizures this time around. This memoir? It has a happy ending. Or at the very least, a soft landing. Because sometimes, just when we need it most, life opens doors for us.

Tulum is such a special place, the land, the ocean, the jungle, the people. There's a pulse there that feels ancient, alive, and deeply healing. I hold it so near and dear to my heart, and I love getting to create memories there with Julian. When we're in Mexico, he's my little jungle boy, wild curls catching the salt air, feet always sandy, giggling as he runs free. No snow boots. No parkas. Just sunshine, fresh fruit, and endless space to explore. In Tulum, we're not just surviving the day. We're living it.

It feels like paradise. But paradise, of course, comes with potholes. Quite literally, the roads are a bumpy adventure of their own, and the craters could probably swallow a small car whole. But you quickly learn that it's just part of the deal. Nowhere is perfect.

There are other little frustrations too, like "Mexico time," where the handyman would say he was coming at 10 a.m. and either never show up or roll in casually around 3 p.m. At first, it drove me crazy, but eventually, I started to loosen my grip. To surrender a little. Time moves differently there, and maybe that's the point of traveling to other places.

I've been all over the world. Chasing magic. Or maybe just remembering that magic is everywhere.

There was Iceland, where the sky rippled with the Northern Lights, in shades of green and violet that brought tears to my eyes. Standing under that glowing sky, it felt like the universe had cracked open just wide enough for me to feel something holy. The air was so still. It was something I had dreamed of since I was small, when I'd learned about the aurora borealis in the movie "Balto." I felt whole and complete and the little girl in me was so happy.

Then there was Bali, where devotion isn't something reserved for temples. It's in the rhythm of daily life, in the gentle sweep of a woman laying petals and incense at her doorstep, in the way strangers smile at you like a familiar friend. Bali reminded me to slow down, to savor the slice of mango and the hush of the early morning light filtering through banana leaves, to not get swept up in the chaos of the moped-flooded streets. To notice. To appreciate. Beauty was everywhere and also within.

In Guatemala, I helped build a school out of plastic water bottles, practiced yoga in the cool stillness of the mornings, and spent my days connecting with the kids in rural Chimaltenango. We didn't share a spoken language, but we didn't need to. Joy was the language. Gratitude, laughter, play, that was how we understood each other. The simplicity of human connection. It was everything. I hold that memory so close to my heart.

Israel is one of those places where, the moment I arrived, I felt it: home. Held. There's something sacred woven into the land itself, like the ground remembers. The energy is ancient and alive all at once. Even the Dead Sea won't let you drown. As though the place itself is reminding you that you're supported.

I know I've been fortunate to have been able to see so much of the world, to witness so much magic. What I've learned along the way though, is that magic doesn't just live in plane tickets and passports.

I used to think I had to travel to far-flung destinations to feel something deeply. Then, I spent a weekend in Milwaukee, an hour-long drive away from home, watching Julian play his own version of fetch with a neighborhood dog at the local playground. His laughter was so full-bodied, so unfiltered, that my eyes welled up just like when I'd seen the Northern Lights. It was a sacred moment, a beautiful memory I'll always hold close to my heart.

And then, as life so often does, it reminded me how quickly everything can shift.

Just as we were getting ready to leave Tulum and return to the states, I started to notice visual changes. "Fuck," I thought to myself, "this is what they were warning me about. This is what we were trying to prevent."

Coming home felt like slamming into a wall. From lush, slow mornings in the jungle to sterile white hallways and chilly exam rooms. No more fresh coconut water, no sand in every crevice of my body. Just fluorescent lights and anxiety.

At the neurosurgeon's office, I knew before he said a word. His face gave it away. The scan showed that the area, once 6 mm, had grown to 24 mm.

What in the actual fuck? It had quadrupled in size.

He was pretty sure it was tumor. My neurologist, on the other hand, was more conservative in her assessment. She thought the scans indicated blood and radiation necrosis. Either way, another surgery, and this time, I didn't cancel. I couldn't. And though they said I was "lucky" to get a spot in just 10 days, I didn't feel lucky. I felt numb. But also calm. Resigned, maybe. Ready.

I had seen what life could look like. I had tasted it, on mountaintops, in jungles, in playgrounds. And that knowing, that memory of joy, stayed with me.

Joy lives in the cracks. In the chaos. In a child's laughter, in the unexpected hug from a stranger. You don't have to go far to find it. You just have to keep your heart open, even when it would be easier to shut it down. Even when your MRI says 24 mm.

The morning of surgery, I was anxious, yes, but strangely, grounded in a way. I brought my squishy tangerine pillow for emotional support. My best friends were praying and sending love from every corner. My boyfriend was there when I woke up. He stayed the night with me in the hospital. I felt safe. Loved. Held.

And then, the results came back: it was blood. A lot of it, about two teaspoons' worth. But no viable tumor.

Thank God. This was the last of the last of it. They didn't even shave that much of my hair off this time. I was grateful. I am grateful.

Life gets to be so fucking good. Peace was here.

I was manifesting a nice, boring rest of the year, toddler birthday parties, baby showers, maybe a few slow Sundays. Mother's Day was right around the corner. I was excited to just be. Boring sounded glorious.

Until, one lovely day at the end of May, I noticed something. My period was three days late.

Not too crazy. But enough to make me pause. Enough to make me take a test, just to calm my nerves.

Positive. Two pink lines. Clear as day. I texted my boyfriend. I didn't start the morning with my usual "Good morning, babe 🤍 " text.

Instead, I wrote: "Can you come by today?"

He called me almost instantly. "Everything okay?"

I took a breath. "I'm pregnant."

EPILOGUE

LIFE RARELY UNFOLDS in the way we planned. But maybe that's the point. You know the saying, "You know how to make God laugh? Tell him your plans."

Apparently, that must mean I am hilarious.

I didn't expect to face brain surgery or a near-death experience in my early thirties. I didn't expect to rebuild my life while raising a toddler, navigating trauma, and rediscovering what it means to feel joy again. I didn't expect to find love in the aftermath, or laughter in the small, quiet moments, like fresh guac in the sun, or my son's giggles while playing on a playground.

Currently I'm manifesting that my biggest problem be a handyman promising to arrive "mañana" only to show up three weeks later holding a mango and zero tools.

These days, I'm envisioning a life that's... delightfully calm. Give me trips to the farmers market, Costco runs, sound baths, yoga, spontaneous dance parties in the kitchen, plenty of snuggles and a full night's sleep (okay, most of a night's sleep).

I don't need chaos to feel alive anymore. I've had enough plot twists to fill a whole damn Netflix series: medical drama meets rom-com meets spiritual awakening. Season 3: Surprise, You're Pregnant!

But here's the thing: I trust myself now. I trust life more. I've learned how to laugh in the hard moments (coping mechanism? Maybe) and cry whenever I need to. I've made peace with not having all the answers. As long as there's love, music, sunshine, and maybe a snack, I'm good.

So no, I don't know exactly what's next. But I do know I'm ready.

Come what may. (Just maybe not all at once, okay Universe?)

ACKNOWLEDGMENTS

IT'S TAKEN ME YEARS to believe in myself that I could actually write this and get this book out there, and I couldn't do it without the support of all of you.

First, to my son Julian, you are my north star, my guiding light. You remind me daily of what truly matters. Thank you for finding me in this lifetime and choosing me to be your mom. You have changed me forever, and for the better.

To my mom, my forever cheerleader. Thank you for your unwavering encouragement, for holding space, and for being there for me every single day. Your love is one of my greatest gifts.

Deep gratitude to Kim, my editor, whose clarity and wisdom shaped this into something far greater than I imagined. Your insight and accountability helped me trust my voice more fully. And thank you Amy, for catching the words I missed and the spaces I overlooked, and for your patience with me.

To my incredible friends, my chosen family: Doris, Kaytlyn, Eliza, Maureen, Jorie, Drake, Lisa, Jamie, Julie, Mathilde, Sophie, Gloria, Marina, Iryna, Monica, Hannah, Olivia, Morgan, Lindsey, Andrew (and anyone else I may have missed). Thank you for showing up for me when I needed you most, for your presence, your laughter, your honesty and unconditional love. You reminded me that I never had to walk this path alone.

To Nathan, thank you for being the reason I'm a mom, and for giving us the greatest blessing of all. Your steady love for Julian means more than words can say. Can always count on you to have new cars handy or a new racetrack or both. I'm grateful for the father you are, and for the friend you've become.

To Aaron: For always being my rock and safe place to land. Thank you for always having the coffee ready, for the way you see me and hold me and make even the mundane feel like magic. Thank you for cheering me on, calming me down and loving me through every wild, messy, beautiful moment. Life's way more fun with you in it, especially as Randy to my Brandy. Here's to always keeping it weird (and wonderful) together.

Thank you to Gary Douglas and Dr. Dain Heer for the energetic contributions and tools that supported my healing.

To the women (and all humans) who've been dismissed, misdiagnosed, overlooked, or told to shrink: I wrote this with you in mind, and I hope it brings you light.

And finally, to the divine timing of it all. I may never understand it, but I am deeply grateful for it.

RESOURCES

If you've made it this far, thank you. Writing this book meant revisiting some of the most difficult and transformative moments of my life. It forced me to sit with memories I once tried to outrun, and to meet myself with more honesty than I thought I could handle.

But it also reminded me how supported I've been, by people, by practices, and by books that found me at just the right time. I'm sharing some of those here in the hopes that they might meet you wherever you are in your own journey. Take what resonates, leave what doesn't. Healing isn't linear, and there's no one right way through.

What matters is that you keep going, in your own way, in your own time.

Breathwork and Meditations

Meditation to Release Tension

Begin by finding a comfortable seat. Feel your sit bones rooting down into the earth, extending your spine long, from the base of your tailbone up through the crown of your head. Notice yourself here. Notice what you notice. Begin by taking a deep breath in through the nose, exhaling fully out through the mouth. Do this two more times. As you exhale, really sigh it out. Now, find a neutral rhythm to your breath and breathe in and out through the nose. Begin to scan your body from head to toe. Notice if there is anywhere you're hanging on to tension and send your breath there. Linger in this spot and with each breath fill that space in your body with a golden light. Allow this light to dissipate the stress or tension you've been carrying. Repeat this exercise anywhere else in your body where you might be carrying stress or tension.

Visualization for Grounding

Begin by finding a comfortable seat, allowing your body to settle into a gentle yet supported pose. Take a slow, deep breath in. Let the air fill your belly, then your lungs, feeling the rise and expansion of your diaphragm, then your chest. As you exhale, let your chest fall and your belly come in to hug your spine. Do this four more times.

Imagine yourself standing in the middle of a serene forest, where the sunlight filters through the trees. Each beam of light dances with the grace of a whispering breeze, inviting you into a world of quiet solitude. As you step forward into this tranquil woodland, feel the soft earth beneath your feet, each step grounding you deeper into this present moment.

With each breath, let the essence of the forest envelop you, a fragrance of pine and earth mixing with the subtle sweetness of that smell after it rains. Allow yourself to become one with this place, breathing in the stillness and exhaling the remnants of your day. Picture yourself walking slowly along a sunlit path, where the worries of yesterday and the uncertainties of tomorrow seem to dissolve into the lush greenery surrounding you.

As you continue your walk, notice the gentle rhythm of your breath, matching the rustling of leaves overhead. This rhythm is a reminder of the simplicity and beauty of now. With each inhalation, draw in the serene energy of this forest, feeling it fill you with a sense of calm and presence. With each exhalation, release any lingering thoughts or distractions, letting them drift away like an occasional leaf that falls softly to the ground.

Find a quiet spot on the path, where a moss-covered log invites you to rest. Sit upon it, feeling this tree beneath you. As you settle in, allow the gentle embrace of the forest to wrap around you, like a warm, supportive hug from the earth.

Here, in this sacred space, reflect on the truth that the present moment is a gift. In the stillness of the forest, with every breath, you notice the beauty of simply being. There are no expectations, no judgments, only the pure experience of being here, fully and completely.

As you sit in this space, take a moment to appreciate the peace that resides within you. Know that this calm is always within you, a space you can return to whenever you need. Let the forest's tranquility infuse you with a profound sense of gratitude for the present moment, and for the opportunity to simply be.

When you feel ready, slowly rise from your resting place, carrying with you the gentle peace of the forest. As you take your final steps back to where this journey first began in the center of the forest, let this experience serve as a reminder that within each moment lies a world of calmness and possibility.

Taking a few deeper breaths in through the nose and out through the mouth, coming back to this time and space. Carry the forest with you, knowing that you can always return to this peaceful space whenever you wish.

Visualization for Peace & Calm

Do this meditation either seated or lying down. You can do this right when you wake up or as you are winding down for bed. If seated, allow your shoulders to soften, rolling them up and away from your ears. Place one hand gently on your belly and the other on your heart. Take a deep breath in through your nose, feeling the air fill your belly and expand your chest. Exhale slowly through your mouth, as though you are blowing out through a straw, allowing your belly to hug toward your spine.

Imagine you are sitting on a quiet beach, the sound of the ocean waves gently rolling in and out. Allow each wave to wash away your thoughts, bringing with it a sense of calm. As you breathe, let your own breath travel in and out with each wave. Inhale in through the nose as the wave comes in, exhale out the mouth as the wave rolls out.

Inhale deeply through your nose, envisioning the rising tide of the sea, lifting your belly as it expands. Feel the gentle stretch and the lightness as your breath flows in. Let this wave of breath bring a sense of openness and awareness.

As you exhale, imagine the tide receding, pulling away from the shore. Feel your belly gently fall, any tension flowing out with the retreating wave. Let go of any stress or tightness as your breath carries you through this wave.

With each inhale, visualize the waves rolling in with a soothing rhythm, lifting and expanding. With each exhale, picture the waves drawing back, leaving you in a state of calm.

Let the motion of your breath be like the ocean's tide: steady, gentle, and unhurried. Your belly rises and falls like the waves, effortlessly and naturally. There is no rush, no struggle, just the natural ebb and flow of your own breath.

Allow your breath to deepen with each cycle. Inhale, letting the waves rise and expand within you. Exhale, allowing the waves to retreat and dissolve any lingering tension. With every breath, you are more attuned to the calming rhythm of the ocean.

Stay with this for a few minutes and notice what you notice, simply being present with the expansion of your belly rising and falling like the ocean waves. Let this feeling of calm and fluidity wash over you, knowing that you carry the peace of the ocean within you.

When you are ready, gently bring your awareness back to the present moment. Wiggle your fingers and toes, stretch if you like, and slowly open your eyes. Carry the calm and rhythmic energy of the ocean with you as you go about your day.

Personal Reflection Prompts

Now that you've read my story, I invite you to reflect on it through your own lens.

- What moments stirred something within you?
- What parts felt familiar?
- Where did you see yourself in my experiences?

One of the most powerful things I've learned through writing this book is just how much clarity and healing can come from looking back with honesty and compassion. When we take the time to reflect, we often uncover patterns, wisdom, and strength we didn't even know we were carrying.

So I encourage you to take a moment for your own story.

- What parts of your journey have shaped who you are today?
- Where are you being called to heal, soften, or rise?
- What chapters would you want to explore more deeply, and why?
- What lessons are asking to be honored or integrated?

ADDITIONAL RESOURCES

The journey of becoming, of healing, growing, and remembering who we are, isn't linear. It meanders, circles back, and unfolds in its own time. Along the way, I've been shaped by the wisdom of so many authors, teachers, and healers whose words found me exactly when I needed them most. The list below includes some of the standout books, practices, and voices that have deeply supported me on my path.

It's not a complete list, because this kind of journey is never really complete. I'm always learning, always discovering something new that lights me up. If you're curious to follow along, I share what's inspiring me in real-time over on Instagram [@rachel.gitlevich]. You're always welcome there.

Conscious Motherhood & Birth

- *Ina May's Guide to Childbirth* by Ina May Gaskin
- *Birthing from Within* by Pam England
- *HypnoBirthing: The Mongan Method* by Marie F. Mongan
- *Go Diaper Free* by Andrew Olson
- The Bradley Method (bradleybirth.com)
- Doula support networks: DONA International

Spiritual & Energetic Practices

- *Many Lives, Many Masters* by Dr. Brian Weiss
- *Women Who Run With the Wolves* by Clarissa Pinkola Estés
- *The Four Agreements* by Don Miguel Ruiz
- *Breath* by James Nestor
- *Braving the Wilderness* by Brené Brown (and pretty much anything by Brené)
- *The Untethered Soul* by Michael A. Singer
- *Start Where You Are* by Pema Chödrön
- *The Celestine Prophecy* by James Redfield

Health and Wellness

- *The Blue Zones* by Dan Buettner
- *SuperLife* by Darin Olien

Inspiration and Motivation

- *The School of Greatness* by Lewis Howes
- *Atomic Habits* by James Clear
- *Think and Grow Rich* by Napoleon Hill
- *Untamed* by Glennon Doyle
- *Greenlights* by Matthew McConaughey
- *Being you Changing the World* by Dr. Dain Heer

www.ingramcontent.com/pod-product-compliance
Lightning Source LLC
Chambersburg PA
CBHW070343130626
46556CB00007B/3001